COMPOSERS
ON
COMPOSERS

COMPOSERS
—ON—
COMPOSERS

JOHN L. HOLMES

GREENWOOD PRESS

New York • Westport, Connecticut • London

Library of Congress Cataloging-in-Publication Data

Holmes, John L.
    Composers on composers / John L. Holmes.
      p.   cm.
    Bibliography: p.
    Includes index.
    ISBN 0–313–26602–6 (lib. bdg. : alk. paper)
    1. Musicians as authors.   2. Composers.   3. Music—History and
criticism.   I. Title.
    ML90.H64   1990
    780′.92′2—dc20   89–11860

British Library Cataloguing in Publication Data is available.

Copyright © 1990 by John L. Holmes

Library of Congress Catalog Card Number: 89–11860
ISBN: 0–313–26602–6

First published in 1990

Greenwood Press, Inc.
88 Post Road West, Westport, Connecticut 06881

Printed in the United States of America

The paper used in this book complies with the
Permanent Paper Standard issued by the National
Information Standards Organization (Z39.48–1984).

10 9 8 7 6 5 4 3 2 1

Contents

Introduction

Composers create worlds of their own, each of which is different from the world of every other composer. Often they are not sympathetic to the music of other composers, finding other styles and musical vocabularies incompatible with their own. A minority have the capacity to be objective and to stand back from their own and others' music and view it all in perspective. Some composers have been music critics at some stages of their lives, but music critics in general, be they composers or not, are not known for their lack of prejudice, especially to new music. It may be unfair to quote assessments of new compositions that composers are hearing for the first time; they are not immune from the general rule that first impressions of new music are usually misleading and that familiarity may reveal its merits.

Selecting the words of composers commenting on other people's music raises additional problems. Not all composers are especially articulate, and some are diffident in offering their opinions. Despite what I have written above, a few are surprisingly tolerant of others; at the other extreme, some condemn almost everything. One of the latter was Frederick Delius, who went so far as to condemn Mozart; Delius was perhaps the only composer, great or otherwise, who thought so little of the Austrian genius. Some composers lived for part of their lives with companions who recorded their every word and prompted them to offer their opinions about other composers and their music, as well as a variety of other subjects. Cosima Wagner's diaries are a constant source of amazement when we read of Richard Wagner's reaction to other music and musicians. Some of his comments are penetrating; others betray the most appalling prejudice. Stravinsky was well recorded by Robert Craft, who made something of an industry out of publishing Stravinsky's *obiter dicta*, but it is often difficult to determine whether Stravinsky's remarks represent a considered opinion or a gentle leg-pull. Shostakovich too has been exhaustively reported by Solomon Volkov, and what was formerly taken for an austere personality emerges from these memoirs as a lively mind, expressing many acid comments about his contemporaries and the world about him—a world replete with perfidy and tragedy. As in his music, Rossini's remarks bubble with humor, although this occasionally was contrived.

Some composer-critics spoke or wrote in English, and then their meaning usually is quite clear. For the rest we have to rely on translations, with all their inaccuracies and limitations. Translating from German to English is notoriously difficult; a word-by-word literal translation results in English that is unreadable if not quite incomprehensible, and the translator has to be given liberty to produce a satisfactory text. This problem is difficult to solve, and in a number of quotations in this book that are translations from German and other languages, the reader may well be surprised at the clumsy style. It is not possible to improve on the translation without close reference to the original, as any alteration to a poor translation, while improving the English, would depart from the meaning of the original.

The remarks of one composer, Hanns Eisler, are included in several places, as they are an instructive example of what has passed for music criticism in countries where Marxist ideology has prevailed. Eisler was a convinced Marxist; for him, therefore, nothing in society, not even music, had an objective existence, and his peculiar Marxist interpretation pervaded all. (Shostakovich was similarly guilty when talking about Scriabin in the early 1930s, at a time when he was under severe political pressure.) Now the political atmosphere in the Soviet Union and Eastern Europe has changed to such an extent that one wonders whether these strictly Marxist attitudes still hold. At least the music of Rachmaninov and other Russian emigré bourgeois composers is played and revered along with the rest.

We can enjoy the wit and wisdom, the curious and the profound comments of composers discussing their fellows. There are also some lessons to learn. Probably the major one is that very little music and very few composers are sacrosanct. Excellent composers with a comprehensive knowledge of music can still have astonishing views about the great masterpieces that today are accepted virtually without criticism by the vast musical public. Vaughan Williams is a good example: his opinion of the slow movement of Beethoven's Ninth Symphony will raise many an eyebrow, as will Verdi's views on the last movement of the same symphony.

Because the comments that follow are personal and hardly definitive, I have chosen to present them in a narrative fashion. Short chapters on seventy-eight composers, organized alphabetically, relate the complimentary or caustic comments of from one to more than twenty of their contemporaneous or later peers, with Beethoven receiving the most attention.

So as not to interrupt the flow of the narrative, the sources of the quotations are documented in a note section following the last chapter. In all, eighty-five composers are quoted, some, notably Mahler, Ravel, and Stravinsky, repeatedly. An index of composers quoted and their subjects completes the work.

This compilation of quotations is not exhaustive for many reasons. There is another book waiting to be written that would compile the views of present-day composers about those of the past. My guess, however, is that what they have to say will never be as interesting as what Tchaikovsky thought of Brahms, Verdi about Wagner, Elgar about Strauss, and so on. In the musical Valhalla where all must be assembled now, there must be some wonderful discussions—that is, if the composers can bear to talk to each other at all.

COMPOSERS
ON
COMPOSERS

Carl Philipp Emanuel Bach
(1714–1788)

The second surviving son of Johann Sebastian Bach and his first wife, Carl Philipp Emanuel Bach, known as the "Hamburg Bach," was an influential teacher and prolific composer who stood midway between the Baroque and Classical periods of music. Mozart was familiar with his music but passed no comment about it in his letters. On the other hand, HAYDN said to Albert Dies after he had discovered C.P.E. Bach's first six piano sonatas: "I did not leave the clavier until I had mastered them all. Innumerable times I played them for my own delight, especially when I felt oppressed and discouraged by worries and always I left the instrument gay and in high spirits."[1]

BEETHOVEN was equally enthusiastic about the sonatas, saying: "I have only a few samples of Emanuel Bach's compositions for the clavier: and yet some of them should certainly be in the possession of every true artist, not only for the sake of enjoyment but also for the purpose of study."[2]

Johann Sebastian Bach
(1685–1750)

Bach and his music were no doubt discussed by his contemporaries, but very few of their comments have been recorded. GIOVANNI BATTISTA MARTINI, known as Padre Martini, who was a composer, writer, and also teacher of Johann Christian Bach, Grétry, and Mozart, wrote three months after Johann Sebastian Bach's death: "I consider it unnecessary to describe the singular merit of Sig. Bach since it is too well known and admired not only in Germany but all over Italy. I will say only that I hold it difficult to find a better *Professore* since every day he can claim to be among the finest in Europe."[3]

Haydn and Mozart were familiar with Bach's music, at least with the preludes and fugues, but in all of MOZART'S letters there is only one reference to Bach, where he remarks to his sister that Baron von Swieten had given him all the works of Handel and Bach to take home with him.[4] Schubert scarcely mentions Bach in his correspondence and recorded conversations. On the other hand, while BEETHOVEN'S greatest admiration was for Handel, his biographer Alexander Wheelock Thayer quotes him as saying: "His name ought not to be Bach [i.e. German for brook] but Ocean, because of his infinite and inexhaustible wealth of combinations and harmonies."[5] In a letter to the Archduke Rudolf, Beethoven also wrote: "Genius was possessed (among the old masters) really only by the German Handel and Sebastian Bach,"[6] and to Breitkopf and Härtel he referred to Bach as "the immortal God of Harmony."[7]

MENDELSSOHN was devoted to the music of Bach, and his performances of the *St. Matthew Passion* in Leipzig in 1829 led to the revival of Bach's music in Germany. In his letters he called Bach "the fountainhead"[8] and reflected on Bach's isolation among his contemporaries and on his "pure, mild and vast power" and the "transparency of the depths."[9] In his room a picture of Bach hung over the piano.[10]

SCHUMANN had the greatest reverence for Bach. In a letter to his mother he wrote:

> Bach's *Well-tempered Clavier* is my grammar—the best there is. I have analysed the fugues one by one in the closest detail, which is of immense value and seems to strengthen one's whole moral fibre. Bach was a real man, a man through and through; there are no half-measures about him, nothing morbid—he composed everything as though for eternity.[11]

He confessed to Clara Wieck: "Bach is my daily bread. I refresh myself in his presence and perpetually draw new ideas from him."[12]

ROSSINI was in awe of Bach, calling him a "colossal creature" and finding it inconceivable that he wrote such a volume of music in such a style: "What is difficult or impossible for others was child's play for him."[13] Bach also had great admirers among French composers; GOUNOD wrote: "Bach is a colossus of Rhodes, beneath whom all musicians pass and will continue to pass. Mozart is the most beautiful, Rossini the most brilliant, but Bach is the most comprehensive: he has said all that there is to say."[14] WAGNER observed to Cosima that some features of Bach's music could only be explained by the fact that he was a great improvisor and that he wrote down what he had been extemporizing. This explained many of the pedantic markings and curious runs.[15]

BRAHMS was once entertained at Cobenzl near Grinzing, outside Vienna. "Yes, gentlemen," observed his host solemnly as the guests sat in almost reverential silence, inhaling the bouquet of some rare wine that had been reserved for the end of the repast, "what Brahms is among composers, so is this Rauenthaler among wines." "Ah then," cried Brahms, "let's have a bottle of Bach now!"[16]

MAHLER often expressed his admiration of Bach, and to make Bach more accessible to the concert-goers of the day he arranged a suite for modern symphony orchestra from movements taken from the Second and Third Suites. He said that he found all the seeds of genius in Bach, much as the world is contained in God,[17] and that he was constantly learning from Bach.[18] He also pointed out that Bach did not concern himself with the originality of his themes, and that "what mattered to him was how to handle them, how to develop and transform them in a multiplicity of different ways." He compared this to the Greeks who took the same subjects for their tragedies and comedies but dealt with them in new and different ways.[19]

Closer to the present day, BARTÓK said:

> The work of Bach is a summing up of the music of some hundred and odd years before him. His musical material is themes and motives used

by his predecessors. We can trace in Bach's music motives, phrases which
were also used by Frescobaldi and many others among Bach's predecessors. Is this plagiarism? By no means. For an artist it is not only right to
have his roots in former times, it is a necesssity.[20]

BRIAN, the British symphonist, wrote in his analysis of the works of
Bach that prefaced the Breitkopf and Härtel catalogue:

> [Bach] remains the most industrious musician who ever lived, yet his great
> choral works were a matter of slow effort, hard thinking, continual re-
> writing and re-shaping. The B Minor Mass, admittedly the greatest choral
> work in existence, occupied Bach almost ten years in its composition.
> When it is considered that Bach never heard his own work in its entirety,
> that it was not even published until 100 years after his death, that so far
> as is known, a complete performance did not take place until 1835, one
> is compelled to reflect on the vagaries of Fate, how it impelled the com-
> poser to deliver great messages which will for ever live with the human
> race, but which Bach himself never had an opportunity of hearing.[21]

STRAVINSKY wrote about the performance of the St. Matthew Passion
in his *Poetics of Music*, which originated as the Charles Eliot Norton Lec-
tures he gave at Harvard University in 1939. According to Robert Craft,
Stravinsky's amanuensis, Stravinsky wrote only 1,500 words of the total
30,000 in the book. A ghost writer, Pierre Souvtchinsky, was responsible
for the rest, so it is not possible to say whether Stravinsky or Souvtchinsky
wrote the following:

> The Saint Matthew Passion of Johann Sebastian Bach is written for a
> chamber-music ensemble. Its first performance in Bach's lifetime was
> perfectly realised by a total force of 34 musicians, including soloists and
> chorus. That is known. And nevertheless in our day one does not hesitate
> to present the work, in complete disregard for the composer's wishes,
> with hundreds of performers, sometimes almost a thousand. This lack of
> understanding of the interpreter's obligations, this arrogant pride in num-
> bers, this concupiscence of the many, betrays a complete lack of musical
> education.[22]

According to Robert Craft again, Stravinsky once exercised his waspish
humor at Bach's expense during an interview: "The only musical hardware
I have examined of late was a musical typewriter which I found to be
marvellously suited to the needs of . . . Bach."[23]

MESSIAEN once remarked that he found Bach's music lacking in
rhythm. While the music has harmonic colors and remarkable contrapuntal
craftsmanship, and while it is marvellous and inspired, it has no rhythm.
He explains that Bach's music may appear rhythmic precisely because it

has no rhythm: "An uninterrupted succession of equal note values plunges the listener into a state of beatific satisfaction; nothing thwarts his pulse, breathing or heartbeats. Thus he is very much at ease, receives no shock, and all this appears to be perfectly 'rhythmic.' "[24]

Mily Balakirev
(1837–1910)

Balakirev was the leader of the "Mighty Five," which consisted of Borodin, Mussorgsky, Cui, Rimsky-Korsakov, and himself. He was an extraordinary musician, as RIMSKY-KORSAKOV testified:

> Balakirev made a great impression on me from the very beginning. He was an excellent pianist, and his capacity for playing at sight and extemporizing was boundless. . . . He had a wide knowledge of music of all kinds and was able to call to mind, at any moment, every bar he had ever heard or read. . . . We were completely bewitched by his talents, his authority, his magnetism.[25]

He was apparently a fine conductor; BORODIN wrote of his conducting of Schumann's Second Symphony: "We have never had anyone who has conducted Schumann's work with such animation, such lucidity and such subtle understanding as Mr. Balakirev. In his conducting even the defects in Schumann's orchestrations are somehow smoothed out."[26] Borodin also wrote, this time to his wife, about Balakirev's piano work *Islamey*: "This piece of music is rather long and confused; the technical side is too obvious; even Balakirev's admirers admit this."[27]

TCHAIKOVSKY was not one of the "Mighty Five" and made this comment:

> Balakirev's personality is the strongest in the whole group. . . . His talent is amazing, but various fatal drawbacks have helped to extinguish it. . . . In spite of his wonderful gifts, he has done a lot of harm. . . . He is the

inventor of all the theories of this extraordinary circle, in which are to be found so many undeveloped, incorrectly developed, or prematurely decayed talents.[28]

Béla Bartók
(1881–1945)

KODÁLY was a fellow Hungarian and a close associate of Bartók. After the first performance of Bartók's Second String Quartet in 1918, Kodály wrote that it is mediocre talent whose development is given towards greater complexity and artificiality, and these composers seek to disguise what they have to say. By contrast, genuine talent strives to discard superficial effects to attain a greater simplicity, and this is the path that Bartók pursued. He added:

> In his constructive understanding of form, Bartók is much more akin to the classical masters, and this essentially new departure is constantly displayed in the [Second] String Quartet. What emerges from the successive movements is not a series of different moods, but the continual evolution of a single, coherent, spiritual process. The impression conveyed by the work as a whole . . . is that of a spontaneous experience.[29]

SIBELIUS said of Bartók: "Bartók was a great genius, but he died in poverty in America. I don't know what he thought about my music, but I always had the highest regard for him."[30] In his preface to Serge Moreux's study of Bartók, HONEGGER wrote:

> Most writers have agreed to hold Schoenberg and Stravinsky responsible for the reaction which set in after Debussy. Some have included Erik Satie; I personally would nominate Bartók instead. These three are authentic representatives of the musical revolution of that generation. Less direct and sparkling than Stravinsky, less dogmatic than Schoenberg, Bartók is perhaps the most profoundly musical of the three and best manifests a close-knit organic development. He had a decided bent towards works

of what are called pure music; one result is that his importance to us is as enduring as that of Schoenberg and Stravinsky, though its impact is less brusque. Not that his music can be grasped at first attempt, for not all performers are capable of rendering it; and its extraordinary rhythmic subtlety calls for a greater effort at precision than does classical music. ... The charge, however, cannot be levelled at the works themselves, for their internal poise is secure and quite convincing.[31]

There is almost nothing recorded in the speech or written word of Stravinsky or Schoenberg about Bartók. This is surprising in the case of Stravinsky, who in the books of his conversations and recollections had much to say about many other composers. Schoenberg is known to have expressed admiration for Bartók, together with other composers as different as Gershwin, Ives, Milhaud, Shostakovich, and Sibelius. When he was president of the famed Society for Private Musical Performances in Vienna in 1918, Schoenberg saw that Bartók's music was included in at least one program.

MESSIAEN drew attention to the place of Hungarian folk music in Bartók's compositions, and to the fact that in his travels through the Hungarian countryside to collect folk songs it was not nature he sought but men. His effort was rewarded because Hungarian folk song is among the loveliest, the most original, and the most varied, and is only surpassed, observed Messiaen, by those of Peru, Bolivia, and Ecuador. He added: "Bartók is a mixture of Hungarian folk-music, academic developments after the manner of fugal episode, and a tendency towards increasingly close-knit chromaticism, very near to serial music."[32]

BLITZSTEIN recognized the dance in Bartók's music:

In Bartók's neo-paganistic music, the moment—laconic, or tumultuous, or beguiling—is everything. The instantaneous effectiveness of his long list of chamber and piano works makes one think of them as being basically theatre-music, even, more specifically, ballet-music. Meditation occurs only during a lull; his lyricism is a singing of the feet.[33]

Ludwig van Beethoven
(1770–1827)

HAYDN encountered the young Beethoven when the latter first came to Vienna, and Beethoven was his pupil for fourteen months. Beethoven was annoyed by Haydn's criticism of his Piano Trios Op. 1; Ferdinand Ries wrote that Haydn had said that he did not believe that the third trio of the set, the one in C Minor, "would be so quickly and easily understood and so favourably received by the public."[34] Haydn, meeting Beethoven in the street once, complimented him on the ballet music Beethoven had written for *The Creatures of Prometheus*; "Oh dear Papa," Beethoven replied, "you are too good, but it is no *Creation* by a long shot." Hearing his greatest work so compared, Haydn retorted: "You are right. It is no *Creation*, and I hardly think it ever will be!"[35] On Haydn's seventy-sixth birthday, in 1808, a performance of *The Creation* was given in his honor at the Vienna University; Beethoven stood with members of the nobility at the door to receive "the venerable guest on his arrival there in Prince Esterhazy's coach." Haydn was carried into the hall in an armchair to the sound of trumpets and drums; Beethoven "knelt down before Haydn and fervently kissed the hands and forehead of his old teacher."[36] After Haydn's death Beethoven always referred to him with the greatest praise and affection, regarding him as the equal of Handel, Bach, Gluck, and Mozart.

WEBER was a contemporary of Beethoven. His famous comment about the Seventh Symphony, cited by Schindler in his biography of Beethoven but subsequently challenged, was: "The extravagances of his genius have reached the *non plus ultra*, and Beethoven must be quite ripe for the madhouse."[37] But a more temperate assessment of Beethoven is also attributed to Weber:

My views differ too much from Beethoven's for me to feel I could ever agree with him. The passionate, almost incredible inventive powers inspiring him are accompanied by such chaotic arrangement of his ideas that only his earlier compositions appeal to me; the later ones seem to me hopeless chaos, an incomparable struggle for novelty, out of which break a few heavenly flashes of genius proving how great he could be if he would tame his rich fantasy.[38]

BERLIOZ had the greatest reverence for Beethoven and described the first impression Beethoven's music made on him: "Hardly had I recovered from the successive shocks of Weber and Shakespeare, when above my horizon burst the sun of glorious Beethoven to melt for me that misty inmost veil of the holiest shrine of music, as Shakespeare had lifted that of poetry."[39] There are many references in Berlioz's memoirs and other writings to Beethoven and his music. Here are some:

Then Beethoven's A Major Sonata, of which the first movement excited us wildly, and the minuet and finale merely redoubled our musical exaltation.[40]

Last night I dreamt of music, this morning I recalled it all and mentally performed the adagio of Beethoven's B Flat symphony. So that little by little I fell into one of those unearthly ecstasies and wept my eyes out at the sound of the tonal radiance which emanates from angels alone.[41]

Theodore Ritter is playing the five concertos of Beethoven in a fortnightly series accompanied by a delightful orchestra. I go and hear these marvels.[42]

So I heard Beethoven's Piano Trio in B Flat, the violin sonata in A and the string quartet in E Minor—the music of the starry spheres. You will understand that after such miracles of inspiration I am in no mood to listen to ordinary music.[43]

This comment by WAGNER about Beethoven is extracted from his vast prose works:

Assuredly there has never been an artist who pondered less upon his art. The brusque impetuosity of his nature shows he felt as an actual personal injury, almost as direct as every other shackle of convention, the ban imposed on his genius by these forms. Yet his rebellion consisted in nothing but the exuberant unfolding of his inner genius, unrestrained by those outward forms themselves. He never did radically alter an existing form of instrumental music; in his last sonatas, quartets, symphonies and so forth, we may demonstrate beyond dispute a structure such as of the first. But compare these works with one another; compare for example the Eighth Symphony in F with the Second in D, and marvel at the wholly new world that fronts us in wellnigh the identical form.[44]

The reverence of LISZT for Beethoven was expressed in these words:

> To us musicians the work of Beethoven parallels the pillars of smoke and fire which led the Israelites through the desert, a pillar of smoke to lead us by day, and a pillar of fire to light the night, so that we may march ahead both day and night. His darkness and his light equally trace for us the road we must follow; both the one and the other are a perpetual commandment, an infallible revelation.[45]

BRAHMS, however, had his reservations, which he expressed in a conversation with Richard Heuberger:

> I understand very well that the new personality of Beethoven, the new outlook, which people found in his works, made him greater, more important in their view [than Mozart's later works]. But 50 years later this judgment has been altered. The attraction of novelty must be differentiated from inner value. I admit that the [Third Piano] Concerto of Beethoven is more modern, but not so important! I am able to undertand, too, that Beethoven's First Symphony did impress people colossally. In fact, it was the new outlook! But the last three symphonies by Mozart are much more important! Some people are beginning to feel that now.[46]

TCHAIKOVSKY went further and wrote in a letter that while he bowed down before the grandeur of some of his compositions, he did not love Beethoven. He explained that his relationship with Beethoven was similar to the way he felt in his childhood towards God, to whom he felt great veneration and fear. But he did not love him, and these sentiments remained unchanged throughout his life. On the other hand, "Christ calls forth exclusively the feeling of love," as he is God, but also Man. Tchaikovsky saw the parallel with Mozart: if Beethoven had a place in his heart analogous to God, he loved Mozart as the musical Christ. He did not think the comparison blasphemous: "Mozart was as pure as an angel, and his music is full of divine beauty."[47]

MAHLER thought that Beethoven could not be understood without realizing what a tremendous revolutionary advance he was compared with his forerunners. Beethoven's achievement can be properly evaluated only if we understand the difference between Mozart's G Minor Symphony and the Ninth: "Of geniuses like Beethoven, of such a sublime and most universal kind, there are only two or three among millions." He could name only three in recent times among poets and composers: Shakespeare, Beethoven, and Wagner.[48]

BRUCKNER, too, stood in awe of Beethoven. After a triumphant performance of his *Te Deum* in Berlin in 1891 he said: "One of the honourable critics wrote that I was a second Beethoven. Good Lord, how could anyone say such a thing?'' And he crossed himself quickly to expunge the possibility of sin.[49]

BUSONI, the Italian pianist and composer, wrote these comments about Beethoven:

> The Latin attitude to art, with its cool serenity and its insistence on outward form, is what refreshes me. It was only through Beethoven that music acquired that growling and frowning expression which was natural enough to him, but which perhaps ought to have remained his lonely path alone. Why are you in such a bad temper, one would often like to ask, especially in the second period.[50]

Another great pianist-composer was the Austrian SCHNABEL (1882–1951). He was especially celebrated for his interpretations of the Beethoven sonatas, of which he performed complete cycles, and he was the first pianist to record all the sonatas and piano concertos. In his autobiography he wrote:

> One can say in the case of Bach, Mozart, Schubert, or Schumann that a considerable portion of their compositions are inferior, measured by their greatest creations. . . . The case of Beethoven is amazing, as nearly *all* his works are of equal greatness. His nine symphonies, his sixteen quartets, almost all of his thirty-two piano sonatas are actually *of the same quality*, even in spite of the fact that they were composed throughout his whole life. Why is it so? Perhaps because he composed fewer works than others? I think that one explanation can be found in the fact that in each new work he wrote, he also faced—or was made by his creative disposition to face—a new formal problem. Each one of his quartets, symphonies and sonatas is decidely different, very definitely different in form, while in that respect Mozart and Bach are rather less varied: unless you investigate the works very closely, it will seem to you that you find the same patterns, the same procedures quite often. Beethoven, I think, was the precursor of all the attempts toward more and more freedom from accepted procedures.[51]

FURTWÄNGLER, the great conductor and profound interpreter of Beethoven, was also a composer. He wrote:

> Scarcely any other German name has been accorded such veneration through the entire world as that of Beethoven. If it is not in the same sense national as the creations of Wagner or Schubert, Beethoven's work yet possesses a spiritual power that Germany does not possess elsewhere in the art of music. Through no one else is the force and greatness of German perception and being brought to such penetrating expression.[52]

EISLER, the German composer and pupil of Schoenberg who migrated to the United States but was forced to leave because of his Communist sympathies and settled in East Germany, wrote this in 1952, in an article titled "Thoughts on the Anniversary of Beethoven's Death": "The greatness of Beethoven's music lies in the character of its expression: pathos without pompousness, heroism without bombast, feeling without sentimentality, compassion without self-indulgence, humor without archness, passion without hysteria."[53]

But there are certain British composers whose attitudes to Beethoven fall somewhat short of adoration. VAUGHAN WILLIAMS wrote: "To this day the Beethoven idiom repels me, but I hope that I have at last learnt to see the greatness that lies behind the idiom I dislike, and at the same time see an occasional weakness behind the Bach idiom I love."[54] BRITTEN said: "I certainly don't dislike all Beethoven, but sometimes I feel I have lost the point of what he's up to. I heard recently the Piano Sonata Op. 111. The sound of the variations was so grotesque that I just couldn't see what they were all about."[55] And DELIUS: "Beethoven's music has never given me a great thrill, though he was, of course, an intellectual giant. I like the symphonies and some of the chamber music, but his choral work I find tedious."[56]

Many composers have commented on specific works of Beethoven. MAHLER said of the First Symphony: "It was Haydn raised to the highest degree of perfection. . . . This fact gave him access to his contemporaries. They could find a link with what they already understood."[57] Cosima Wagner recounted in her diary that WAGNER encountered a group of poor blind musicians in a courtyard who were playing the Larghetto of Beethoven's Second Symphony "so wonderfully that he would not tear himself away from them, and he told me about it with tears in his eyes."[58] DONALD FRANCIS TOVEY, the English pianist, composer, conductor, and critic, was one of the most perceptive writers about the music of Beethoven and other composers. He said of the same movement, the Larghetto, of the Second Symphony: "The larghetto is one of the most luxurious slow movements in the world. . . . To many a musical child, or child in musical matters, this movement has brought about the first awakening to a sense of beauty in music."[59]

WAGNER's admiration of the Third Symphony, the *Eroica*, was unbounded. When reading the score with Cosima once, he exclaimed: "The only mortal who can be compared to Shakespeare!"[60] He also remarked that it was the C Sharp of the first theme of the *Eroica* that represents all modern music: "Who else, either before or after Beethoven, could have uttered this sigh within the complete calm of a theme?"[61] BAX, the English symphonist, has been quoted as saying: "The first movements of the *Eroica* and Ninth Symphonies represent the ultimate in symphonic thought and construction."[62]

SCHUMANN'S famous description of the Fourth Symphony was that it is like "a slender Greek maiden between two Norse giants."[63] BER-

LIOZ'S feeling for the first movement of the symphony was very remark-able:

> One is seized, from the first bars, with an emotion that by the end becomes shattering in its intensity!... the impression produced is like that one experiences on reading the touching episode of Francesca da Rimini in the *Divina Commedia*, of which Virgil could not hear the recital without sobbing and weeping, and which, in the last verse, made Dante fall as if dead.[64]

WAGNER said of the Fourth Symphony that it contained the "unworried mood" that was first evident in the *Eroica* and the string quartets and that rose to a "godlike humor," a predecessor of the Eighth Symphony.[65]

In his memoirs BERLIOZ mentions a discussion with his teacher Lesueur at the Paris Conservatoire regarding the Fifth Symphony. Lesueur said to him: "All the same, music like that ought not to be written." Berlioz retorted: "Don't worry, master, there is not much danger that it will."[66] Both WAGNER and MAHLER spoke of the difficulty in conducting the first movement of the Fifth Symphony. Cosima recorded in her diary that Richard "would like to change the [2/4] time signature of the first movement into 4/4 because it is so awkward to beat as it is written, and the nuances suffered in this rhythm."[67] MAHLER remarked that it would have been easier to maintain the rigorous tempo of the first movement if Beethoven had emphasized each of the hammer strokes of the first notes with kettledrums, as the orchestra would have to play in perfect unison. When rehearsing the orchestra, he said that the first notes resembled a violent assault, and that the first movement must be played with "frenzy and stormy restlessness." But he thought that only Beethoven's First, Second, and Fourth Symphonies were well performed by contemporary conductors and orchestras, and that the other symphonies were beyond them. Mahler added that before himself only Wagner was faithful to Beethoven's spirit.[68]

TOVEY wrote:

> This work [the Fifth Symphony] shares with Beethoven's Seventh Symphony the distinction of not only being the most popular but also among the least misunderstood of musical classics.... Mistakes and misreadings in this mighty work have been as frequent as anywhere... but not even the notorious old trick of changing the first three quavers into crotchets has been able to make any headway against the overwhelming power and clearness of the whole.[69]

PARRY discussed the Scherzo of the Fifth Symphony:

> The whole of the Scherzo of the C Minor Symphony is as near being miraculous as human work can be; but one of the most absorbing moments

is the part where, for fifteen bars, there is nothing going on but an insignificant chord continuously held by low strings and a *pianissimo* rhythmic beat of the drum. Taken out of its context, it would be perfectly meaningless. As Beethoven has used it, it is infinitely more impressive than the greatest noise Meyerbeer and his followers ever succeeded in making.[70]

SPOHR, who was a contemporary of Beethoven, wrote in his autobiography about a performance of the Fifth Symphony he heard at a concert in Munich in 1815:

> The effect was even greater than my anticipations, although I had already frequently heard the work in Vienna, under Beethoven's own direction. Notwithstanding the splendor of the execution, however, I found no reason to depart from my original judgment of the work. With all its individual beauties it does not form a classical whole. In particular the theme of the first movement is wanting in the dignity which, in my mind, is indispensable for the opening of a symphony. Putting this aside, the subject, being short and intelligible, is well adapted for contrapuntal working, and is combined with other chief ideas of the movement in a most ingenious and effective manner. The Adagio in A Flat is in parts very beautiful; but the same progressions and modulations recur so often, though each time with more florid expression, that one is at length wearied by them. The Scherzo is most original and thoroughly romantic in color, but the Trio, with its blustering double basses, is too grotesque for my taste. The last movement pleased me least of all by its unmeaning babel; but the return of the Scherzo in the Finale is so happy an idea that one cannot but envy the composer for it. The effect is ravishing! Pity that all the empty noise should come back and efface the impression![71]

TOVEY epitomized the Sixth Symphony, the *Pastoral*: "The Pastoral Symphony has the enormous strength of someone who knows how to relax."[72] BERLIOZ referred to the symphony as "this astonishing landscape [which] seems as if it were the joint work of Poussin and Michelangelo."[73] Of all Beethoven's symphonies the *Pastoral* appeared to be MAHLER'S favorite; he said: "In order to understand it one must have a *feeling for nature*, which most people lack."[74] SCHUMANN commented on the pictorial aspect of the work:

> Beethoven understood the danger he ran in his Pastoral Symphony. In the few words with which he headed it, "Rather expressive of the feeling than tone-painting," lies an entire aesthetic system for composers. But how absurd it is in painters to make portraits of him sitting beside a brook, his head in his hands, listening to the bubbling water![75]

WAGNER called the Seventh Symphony "the Apotheosis of the Dance; the Dance in its highest condition; the happiest realisation of the movements of the body in an ideal form.''[76] TOVEY wrote of the symphony as one of Beethoven's greatest works, echoing Beethoven's own remark to Salomon in 1815, "A grand Symphony in A, one of my best works," and in another letter to Neste, "Among my best works which I can boldly say of the Symphony in A.''[77] WAGNER was puzzled by the contrasts in the symphony:

> But compare the roughness of the opening and concluding movements of this work with the grace, loftiness and even deep devotional feeling of its middle sections, and we are presented with similar puzzling contrasts to those so often found in Beethoven's life, where, in his journals and letters, we find religious and personal appeals to God, worthy of one of the Hebrew Psalmists, side by side with nicknames and jokes which befit a harlequin.[78]

WEINGARTNER'S observations about the Seventh Symphony are from the point of view of the interpreter:

> This is one of the strangest pieces Beethoven has written. The themes in themselves are anything but beautiful; indeed, they are almost insignificant. Small variety in the rhythm, no trace of polyphony, modulations such as any composer can produce, and yet this extraordinary effect which cannot be compared with that of any other piece. It is an unexampled bacchanalian orgy!—To reproduce it impressively is, in my opinion, one of the greatest tasks of the conductor—not indeed in its technical, but in its spiritual bearing.[79]

SPOHR described in his autobiography Beethoven conducting a performance of the Seventh Symphony at a concert that he attended:

> At this concert I first saw Beethoven conduct. Often as I had heard of it, it surprised me extremely. He was accustomed to convey the marks of expression to the band by the most peculiar motions of his body. Thus at a *sforzando* he tore his arms, which were before crossed on his breast, violently apart. At a *piano* he crouched down, bending lower the softer the tone. At the *crescendo* he raised himself by degrees until at the *forte* he sprang up to his full height; and without knowing it, would often at the same time shout aloud.[80]

When Beethoven was told that his Eighth Symphony was not the success of the Seventh, he said: "That's because it is so much better."[81] In the nineteenth century performances were given of the Eighth Symphony with its Allegretto replaced by the Allegretto of the Seventh Symphony. But today we recognize the complete work, to quote WEINGARTNER, as "one of his most mature masterpieces, the instrumentation [reaching] a wonderful degree of perfection."[82] Cosima wrote in her diary that WAG-

NER considered the Seventh and Eighth Symphonies "incomparably the boldest and most original [of the symphonies]; however if he himself were ever to conduct them again he would not hesitate to change some of the things in the orchestration, which Beethoven had written thus only because he could no longer hear it."[83]

The Ninth Symphony has brought all manner of comment from many composers. SPOHR wrote this in his autobiography, which gives yet another idea how Beethoven's music impressed his contemporaries:

> Up to this period [1813], there was no noticeable falling off in Beethoven's creative powers; but from this time onward, owing to his constantly increasing deafness, he could no longer hear any music, which needs must have had a prejudicial effect upon his imagination. His constant endeavour to be original and to open up new paths could no longer be preserved from error by the guidance of his ear, as before. Was it, then, to be wondered at that his works became more and more eccentric, disconnected and incomprehensible? True, there are people who fancy that they can understand them and who, taking pleasure in this, rank them far above his early masterpieces; but I am not of their number, and I freely confess that I have never been able to enjoy these last works of Beethoven. Yes, I must even include the much admired Ninth Symphony among them, the first three movements of which, in spite of some isolated flashes of genius, are to my mind inferior to all the eight previous symphonies. The fourth movement is in my opinion so monstrous and tasteless, so trivial in its grasp of Schiller's Ode, that I can never bring myself to understand how a genius like Beethoven could have written it. I find in it another proof of what I had already noticed in Vienna—that Beethoven is lacking in aesthetic feeling and in a sense of beauty.[84]

At the other extreme, RACHMANINOV declared, a century later, "Nobody will ever write anything better than this symphony."[85] Earlier, in 1871 to be exact, BIZET wrote in a letter: "Beethoven is not a man, he is a God!—Like Shakespeare, like Homer, like Michelangelo!—Take the most intelligent public, let them listen to the greatest work in modern art, the Ninth Symphony, and they will understand nothing."[86]
And DEBUSSY:

> Nothing is superfluous in this stupendous work, not even the Andante, declared by modern aestheticism to be over long; is it not a subtly conceived pause between the persistent rhythm of the Scherzo and the instrumental flood that rolls the voices irresistibly onward to the glory of the Finale? . . . The flood of human feeling which overflows the ordinary bounds of the symphony sprang from the soul drunk with liberty, which, by the ironical decree of fate, beat itself against the gilded bars within which the misdirected charity of the great had confined him. Beethoven must have suffered cruelly in his ardent longing that humanity should find

utterance through him; hence the call of his thousand-voiced genius to the humblest and poorest of his brethren. Did they hear it? That is the question.[87]

Debussy also had these observations about the future of the symphony after Beethoven:

A symphony is always received with enthusiasm. It seemed to me that after Beethoven the uselessness of the symphony was proved. Neither with Schumann nor Mendelssohn is it anything more than a respectful but already less forceful repetition of the same forms. Still, the "Ninth" is a model of genius, showing a magnificent desire to enlarge and liberate the accustomed forms by giving them the harmonious measurements of a fresco.

The true lesson taught by Beethoven, then, was not to preserve the old forms, nor an obligation to set our feet in the imprints of his earliest footsteps. It was to look out of open windows upon the free heavens. But it seems to me that they have been shut for ever: the few successes attained by men of genius with this species do little to excuse the studied and factitious exercises which are habitually described as symphonies.[88]

In his essay on Beethoven (1870), WAGNER argued that the importance of the last movement of the symphony comes from the character of the human voice rather than the sentiments it expresses. In the great melody of the last movement

we see the master steadily remaining in music. . . . for in truth it is not the meaning of the Word that engages us at the entry of the human voice, but the character of the voice itself. Nor is it the thought expressed in Schiller's verses that henceforth occupies us, but the intimate timbre of the choral song, in which we feel ourselves invited to join in, and so take part as a kind of congregation in an ideal divine service, as was the case at the entry of the chorale in the Passions of Bach. It is quite evident, especially in regard to the main melody, that Schiller's words have been tacked on arbitrarily and with little skill: for the melody had first of all unfolded itself in all its breadth before us as a thing in itself, given to the instruments alone, and there had filled us with a nameless feeling of joy in a paradise regained.[89]

But VERDI had his reservations about the last movement:

The alpha and omega is Beethoven's Ninth Symphony, marvellous in the first three movements, very badly set in the last. No one will ever approach the sublimity of the first movement, but it will be an easy task to write as badly for voices as is done in the last movement.[90]

VAUGHAN WILLIAMS, too, demurred, but his point of criticism was the Adagio, the third movement:

> When I admit that this symphony is an unapproachable masterpiece, I do not mean that I accept as perfect every note, every phrase, every chord; perhaps even I do not consider it in every detail a model work of art. . . . For me there are certain passages in the Ninth Symphony which I find hard to swallow, but I do not include in this indigestible matter the choral finale, though even here there are certain things which stick in my gizzard. . . . Again, is not the second subject of the third movement, though charming as a *morceau de salon*, quite out of keeping with the unearthly grandeur of the work as a whole?"[91]

STRAVINSKY also reflected on the last movement:

> The failure of the last movement must be attributed, in large measure, to its thumping theme. As the composer cannot develop it—who would?— he spreads it out like a military parade. I am ever surprised in this movement by the poverty of the *Allegro ma non tanto*, as well as the riches of the *Allegro energico* (especially measures 70–90, which, oddly enough, anticipate Verdi). I am undoubtedly wrong to talk this way about "The Ninth", of course, or to question "what everyone knows". "The Ninth" is sacred, and it was already sacred when I first heard it in 1897. I have often wondered why. Can it have something to do with a "message" or with so-called proletarian appeal?[92]

The first impression of the Ninth Symphony on the young WAGNER was overwhelming:

> As my musical instruction . . . did me no good, I continued in my wilful process of self-education by copying out the scores of my beloved masters. . . . Beethoven's Ninth Symphony became the mystical goal of all my strange thoughts and desires about music. I was first attracted to it by the opinion prevalent among musicians, not only in Leipzig but elsewhere, that this work had been written by Beethoven when he was already half mad. It was considered the *non plus ultra* of all that was fantastic and incomprehensible, and this was quite enough to rouse in me a passionate desire to study this mysterious work. At the very first glance at the score, of which I obtained possession with such difficulty, I felt irresistibly attracted by the long-sustained pure fifths of which the first phase opens: these chords . . . seemed in this case to form the spiritual keynote of my own life.[93]

Later, in a letter to Liszt (1855) Wagner made his observation about the last movement of the Ninth Symphony:

In the Ninth Symphony the last choral movement is decidedly the weakest part, although it is historically important, because it discloses to us in a very naive manner the difficulties of a real musician who does not know how . . . he is to represent paradise.[94]

Finally, regarding the Ninth Symphony, DEBUSSY, for one, defended the last movement:

Beethoven wanted this idea [the theme of the finale] to be fraught with its potential development: and of wondrous beauty in itself it is magnificent for the things it foreshadows. There is no example of a more ductile musical idea or of one more triumphantly led whither it is destined to go. It dashes from joy to joy, it never seems to tire, nor to repeat itself; imagine some magical tree suddenly unfolding all its leaves at once.[95]

Other works of Beethoven have attracted fewer comments. MAHLER said this of the *Missa Solemnis*: "I didn't understand it myself to begin with, the Credo least of all. . . . Beethoven proclaimed the Credo in a strange way, with a sort of rage: 'I believe because it's absurd to believe' whereas Bach did so quite differently, with confidence and trust."[96] Cosima recorded in her diary WAGNER's comment on the first movement of the Piano Sonata No. 29, the *Hammerklavier*: "Richard says he knows of no symphonic movement, with the exception of perhaps the first movement of the *Eroica*, that is more effectively carried out; it seems like a play of the most tremendous imagination, containing everything—longing, pain, joy, everything."[97] Wagner described in his autobiography how he became infatuated at an early age with Beethoven's song *Adelaide*, "whose tender refrain seemed to me the symbol of all loving appeals."[98] But Debussy said that it was a piece "which the old Master must have forgotten to burn."[99]

We conclude with STRAVINSKY'S affirmation about the last quartets of Beethoven. He said that they were the highest articles of his musical belief and were "indispensable to the ways and means of art as a musician . . . thinks of art and has tried to learn it, as temperature is to life."[100]

Vincenzo Bellini
(1801–1835)

WAGNER's admiration of Bellini was expressed in an article that he published anonymously when he was in Riga in 1837. It was intended to stimulate interest in *Norma*, which Wagner was then to present.

> What enchants us is the limpid melody, the simple, noble, lovely song of Bellini. It is surely no sin to confess this and to believe in it; perhaps even it would not be a sin if before we went to sleep we were to pray to Heaven that some day German composers might achieve such melodies and such an art in handling song. Song, Song, and yet again Song, ye Germans![101]

Although Wagner thought Bellini's music "utterly insignificant," he found in it "the warm glow of life" which the German operatic music of the day lacked.[102]

After Bellini's death at the age of thirty-four, ROSSINI commented that he was at his greatest in *Norma* and *I puritani*. While his spirit was beautiful and exquisitely delicate, Rossini said, ideas did not come to him in abundance. But as he died when he was still young and at the most beautiful point of his artistic life, he had not had time to display himself to the full.[103] VERDI, too, understood Bellini's weakness in his instrumentation and his harmonic writing, but recognized his richness of feeling and "a certain personal melancholy, which is completely his own."[104]

Alban Berg
(1885–1935)

SCHOENBERG was Berg's teacher and wrote of his surprise that Berg, who was a soft-hearted and timid young man, had the courage to write *Wozzeck*, a drama of such tremendous tragedy that it seemed difficult to express in music and invited disaster. In addition, the opera had episodes of everyday life, contrary to the conception of opera that still then was of conventional characters and stylized costumes. But, said Schoenberg, Berg succeeded, and *Wozzeck* was one of opera's greatest successes. The reason was that Berg was a "strong character who was faithful to his ideas," just as he was faithful to Schoenberg even when he was discouraged from studying with him. "Making the belief in ideas one's destiny is the great quality which makes the great man."[105]

Schoenberg also pointed out that Berg was the least orthodox of the three—Schoenberg, Berg, and Webern—as he combined in his operas pieces or parts of pieces that were distinctly tonal with pieces that were distinctly nontonal. Berg was apologetic in his explanation for this, saying that he could not renounce the contrast offered by the change from major to minor for dramatic expression and characterization. Schoenberg added that while Berg was wrong theoretically, he was right as a composer.[106]

Schoenberg wrote that after he had left Vienna for Berlin in 1911, Berg was left to his own devices and then wrote his String Quartet. This work surprised him unbelievably by "the fullness and unconstraint of its musical language, the strength and sureness of its presentation, its careful working and significant originality. . . . He has shown that he was equal to the task."[107]

BOULEZ, who is both a spiritual and technical descendent of Schoenberg, has said that it was Berg's complexity that struck him. His music is a "universe in perpetual motion" that turns on itself. Berg makes numerous references to himself, his musical construction is very intricate, and his texture is dense.[108]

SHOSTAKOVICH said that Mahler and Berg were his favorite composers, and that he liked *Wozzeck* very much and would never miss a performance of it when it was presented in Leningrad.[109] JANÁČEK was distressed when *Wozzeck* was withdrawn after only several performances at the Prague National Theatre in 1929 because of the demonstrations that then occurred: "Injustice—injustice to *Wozzeck* and a grave injustice to Berg. He is a dramatist of great seriousness and deep truth. Let him speak! Today he is distraught. He suffers. Stopped in his tracks. Not another note. And each of his notes has been dipped in blood."[110] When the conductor Jascha Horenstein performed *Wozzeck* in Paris in 1950, BOULEZ tried to attend every one of the fifteen orchestral rehearsals. He said that he found the opera more and more remarkable in its complexity, which was sometimes indecipherable. It made him "exult beyond belief."[111]

Surprisingly, GERSHWIN admired Berg and said this of the *Lyric Suite*: "Although this quartet is dissonant . . . it seems to me that the work has genuine merit. Its conception and treatment are thoroughly modern in the best sense of the word."[112]

Hector Berlioz
(1803–1869)

SCHUMANN, a redoubtable critic, was one of the first to recognize the genius of Berlioz. In his review of the *Symphonie fantastique* he wrote: "Berlioz does not try to be pleasing and elegant.... What he loves, he almost crushes in his fervour."[113] Schumann traced the principal motif of the symphony: its initial appearance in the first movement, the screaming chords in C Major in the second movement, the development of a new rhythm and harmonies in the trio, its appearance as a recitative in the third movement, its interruption by the orchestra taking on the expression of a dreadful passion after which it seems to collapse in a swoon, its role in the *Marche au supplice* when it is cut off by the *coup fatal* when it tries to speak again, and then its use in the last movement, the *Witches' Sabbath*, when its appearance in the clarinet is "withered, degraded, and dirty."[114]

WAGNER heard Berlioz's large instrumental works in the winter of 1839–40 and was most impressed by them. "The fantastic daring, the sharp precision with which the boldest combinations—almost tangible in their clearness—impressed me, drove back my own ideas of the poetry of music with brutal violence into the very depths of my soul."[115] In the *Romeo and Juliet* symphony he "found a great deal that was empty and shallow...a work that lost much by its length and form of combination."[116] But he found the "musical genre-pictures woven into the [*Symphonie fantastique*] ...particularly pleasing," *Harold in Italy* delighted him in every respect, and the *Grande symphonie funèbre et triomphale* "thoroughly convinced [him] of the greatness and enterprise of this incomparable artist."[117] However, WAGNER was anything but impressed by Berlioz as a conductor when he heard him conduct a Mozart symphony: "I . . . was amazed to find a conductor, who was so energetic in the interpretation of his own compositions, sink into the commonest rut of the vulgar time-beater."[118]

MENDELSSOHN also heard Berlioz conduct the *Symphonie fantastique*, but he found the work dreadfully slow and described it as "insipid and lifeless."[119] In a letter to Moscheles, Mendelssohn wrote about the overture *Les Francs juges*: "His orchestration is such a frightful muddle . . . that one ought to wash one's hands after handling one of his scores."[120]

VERDI remarked in 1882 that Berlioz was a poor sick man, angry with the world. His talent was great, and he had a flair for instrumentation, anticipating Wagner in many orchestral effects. But he lacked the moderation and calm that is necessary for complete works of art. "He always went to extremes, even when creating something praiseworthy."[121] On another occasion VERDI said that he knew Berlioz well and regarded him as a great man, although not everybody could understand his music. He thought that *La Damnation de Faust* was his masterpiece.[122]

LISZT'S relationship with Berlioz was long and went through many phases. He transcribed the *Symphonie fantastique*, *Harold in Italy*, and other pieces for piano and led the first performance of *Benvenuto Cellini* after its disastrous première in Paris. In a letter to Wagner, LISZT wrote: "Of all contemporary composers he is the one with whom you can converse in the simplest, openest and most interesting manner. . . . He is splendid in his ardour and warmth of heart, and I confess that even his violence delights me."[123]

BIZET was an ardent advocate for Berlioz and once stoutly defended him at a gathering he attended. A performance of part of *Les Troyens* in Paris in 1864, which was something of a shambles because the singers forgot their parts and there were mishaps with the scene shifting, caused a violent controversy that nearly involved Bizet in fighting a duel. Bizet once compared Berlioz with Auber: "Auber, who had so much talent and so few ideas, was nearly always understood, while Berlioz, who had genius without talent, almost never was."[124]

DEBUSSY said that Berlioz was "a tremendous humbug, I believe, that managed to believe in his own hoaxes."[125] RAVEL wrote to M. D. Calvocoressi that he had little to admire in the music of Berlioz. While he praised his innovative orchestral technique, he often found his harmony clumsy, observing once that he was "a genius who couldn't harmonise a waltz correctly."[126] RICHARD STRAUSS, in a letter to Cosima Wagner, described Berlioz as "one of the most significant personalities in the history of art."[127] He also wrote in an earlier letter to Cosima regarding *La Grande Messe des Morts*:

> I think it is the richest creation of this unique genius and the most important work in the field of church music except [Beethoven's] *Missa Solemnis* and Liszt's *Grand Mass*. The wealth of ideas of genius, which

one is accustomed to, after all, in this original artist, is combined here with a profundity of emotion of which I know few examples in Berlioz's works. At the side of a gigantic work like that, a German Requiem by that canting, abstemious Temperance-Leaguer Brahms looks puny indeed.[128]

About *Les Troyens*, Strauss wrote in a letter to his father: "A mixture of stupefying nonsense and spine-tingling genius, the frantic struggles of a musician of genius to find the most profound, emotional expression, combined with absolute blindness for the stage and dramatic construction."[129] Describing Dido's love scene (the Royal Hunt and Storm), Strauss wrote in the same letter that Berlioz had "written music of such fabulous beauty and magical sound [that I] forgot the entire nonsense on the stage."[130]

STRAVINSKY (or was it his ghost writer Pierre Souvchinsky?) wrote in his *Poetics of Music*: "[Berlioz's] prestige is great. It can be attributed above all to the *brio* of his orchestra that evidences the most disquieting originality, an originality entirely gratuitous, without foundation, one that is insufficient to disguise the poverty of invention."[131] MESSIAEN admired Berlioz as an orchestrator, calling him "the father of modern orchestration," who made composers aware of the role of timbre, as he was the first to understand the specific timbre of each instrument. Before Berlioz, Messiaen observed, timbres were interchangeable.[132] But not VAUGHAN WILLIAMS: "The only two composers, as far as I know, who never used an instrument when composing were Berlioz and Rheinberger. Comment is unnecessary."[133]

Georges Bizet
(1838–1875)

Bizet's *Carmen* has been regarded by almost all other composers as a masterpiece, perhaps the ideal opera. MAHLER called it "absolute perfection," and when he conducted it, he said that he experienced a profound happiness, finding new qualities in it every time. Josef Förster once asked MAHLER to lend him a score of *Die Meistersinger* so that he could study its polyphony and instrumentation; Mahler replied that the opera was, in his opinion, badly orchestrated and that he preferred *Carmen*, in which, he said, "not a single superfluous note is to be found."[134] BRAHMS went to hear *Carmen* twenty times and is reported to have said that he would have gone to the ends of the earth to embrace Bizet.[135] VAUGHAN WILLIAMS wrote in his autobiography: "I went to *Carmen*, prepared to scoff, but . . . I remained to pray."[136] TCHAIKOVSKY considered *Carmen* a masterpiece and one of those rare compositions that reflect the musical aspirations of an entire epoch. He said that it was delightful and charming from beginning to end, and that he could not play the last scene without weeping.[137]

Other composers who were admirers of *Carmen* include Wagner, Gounod, Busoni, Debussy, Saint-Saëns, Puccini, Delius, Grieg, and Prokofiev. The one dissenting voice was STRAVINSKY, who called the opera "a most inferior work, the summit of banality."[138]

Ernest Bloch
(1880–1959)

BLITZSTEIN wrote of Ernest Bloch, the Swiss-born American composer: "Bloch is a Post-Impressionist, his world the dim internal world of recreated sense-experience, his austerities a sort of sensual abstinence, his marked Hebraism elaborate, infused, and decorative: it is religious more than racial."[139]

Arrigo Boito
(1842–1918)

In addition to being the composer of *Mefistofele* and *Nerone*, Boito was the librettist for VERDI'S *Otello* and *Falstaff*. Verdi wrote of him:

> It's hard to say now whether Boito will ever endow Italy with any masterpieces. He has great talent, he aspires to be original, but he succeeds only in being strange. He lacks spontaneity and he lacks the real incentive: much musical quality. With such tendencies one may succeed more or less with so strange and theatrical a subject as *Mefistofele*, with *Nero* it's more difficult.[140]

Alexander Borodin
(1833–1887)

Borodin's devotion to chemistry and the women's movement in Russia and his great charity in providing accommodation in his house for relatives and poor people prevented him from composing except for a few works. RIMSKY-KORSAKOV deplored this, writing:

> Owing to his infinite kindness and his entire lack of self-love, these surroundings made it extremely inconvenient for him to work at composition. One might come again and again and keep demanding how much he had written. New result—a page or two of score, or else—nothing at all. To the query: "Alexander Porfiryevich, have you done the writing?" he would reply: "I have." And then it would turn out that the writing he had done was a batch of letters! "Alexander Porfiryevich, have—you—finally—transposed such and such a number of the opera score?"—"Yes, I have"—he replies earnestly. "Well, thank the Lord! at last!"—"I transposed it from the piano to the table"—he would continue with the same earnestness and composure![141]

TCHAIKOVSKY also made much the same point:

> He has talent, even a strong one, but it has perished through neglect, because of a blind *fate* which led him to a chair of chemistry instead of into the living profession of music. . . . His technique is so weak that he cannot write a single line without outside help.[142]

Even so, Rimsky-Korsakov had a better opinion of Borodin the musician than Tchaikovsky, writing: "He was better informed than me on the practical side of orchestration, as he played the cello, oboe and flute."[143]

SHOSTAKOVICH remarked that *Prince Igor* was as much Borodin's as it was Rimsky-Korsakov's and Glazunov's, although the latter two tried to conceal the fact, saying that Glazunov wrote down this and that section from memory. But, Shostakovich said, when Glazunov was in his cups he would admit that he simply wrote the overture for Borodin. In fact, it does not often occur that a composer writes excellent music for another and will not admit it.[144]

Pierre Boulez
(b. 1925)

Boulez's teacher at the Paris Conservatoire, MESSIAEN, said that Boulez is the greatest musician of his generation, although he said that he is very far from his own musical universe. Not only is he the greatest composer of serial music, but in Messiaen's estimation he is the only one, and he sees him as his successor in the field of rhythm, taking from Messiaen the idea of rhythmic unease and the idea of rhythmic research. He also used rhythmic formulae derived directly from Greek and Indian music.[145]

Several of Boulez's contemporaries are less certain of his place in the musical history of this century. STRAVINSKY said of Boulez's composition *Pli selon pli*: "Pretty monotonous and monotonously pretty."[146] BERNARD HERRMANN, composer of film music, was even more rueful:

> I don't see any use to write a language no one understands. I don't understand Boulez—last month in London he said, "I will never conduct Tchaikovsky, Strauss or Puccini." I suppose the crap he's doing is better. I mean, he's a talented man, but he doesn't have any feeling.[147]

Johannes Brahms
(1833–1897)

It was SCHUMANN who first hailed the young Brahms when he was unknown at the age of twenty. Writing in *Neue Zeitschrift für Musik* in a commentary headed "New Paths," he declared that there was then a fresh impetus in music coming from the presence of a number of young talents. One must inevitably appear, he went on, who would be destined to give expression to the highest ideals of the times, and who would reveal his mastery gradually as he developed his full powers. Schumann then wrote:

> Seated at the piano he [Brahms] began to disclose most wondrous regions. It was also most wondrous playing, which made of the piano an orchestra of mourning or jubilant voices. There were sonatas, more like disguised symphonies; songs whose poetry would be intelligible even to one who did not know the words, although a profound vocal line flows through them all; a few piano pieces, partly of a demonic character, charmingly formed; the sonatas for violin and piano, string quartets, etc.—all so different one from another that seemed to flow from a separate source. And finally it seemed as though he himself, a surging stream incarnate, swept them all together into a single waterfall, sending aloft a peaceful rainbow above the turbulent waves, flanked on the shores by playful butterflies and the voices of nightingales.[148]

Later, German music was riven into two camps, each owing allegiance to either Wagner or Brahms. Brahms had little animosity towards Wagner and admired much of his music, but Wagner, on the other hand, had nothing but condescension and scorn for Brahms and his music. In the entire 887 pages of WAGNER'S *My Life* there is only one mention of

Brahms, describing a time when he met the latter: "Brahms' behaviour proved unassuming and good-natured, but he showed little vivacity and was often hardly noticed at our gatherings."[149]

In Cosima Wagner's diaries from 1869 to 1877, which cover all of 1,010 pages in the English translation, Brahms is mentioned very few times, and then only disparagingly. Once, in August 1874, Cosima writes that Brahms is described in intimate conversation with friends as having "a bigoted influence on the educated middle classes."[150] Later, in November 1875, Cosima and Richard heard Brahms play on his Piano Quartet in C Minor, Op. 60; Cosima describes it as "very dry and stilted," and Brahms himself as "a red crude-looking man."[151] It would be surprising if Cosima's opinion of Brahms differed from that of her husband's.

WOLF was one of the Wagner camp. "The true test of the greatness of a composer," he said, "is this—*can he exult*? Wagner can exult; Brahms cannot." He wrote:

> Brahms is an epigone of Schumann and Mendelssohn. He is a clever musician, very skilled in counterpoint, to whom ideas of all kinds come— sometimes good, now and then excellent, occasionally bad, here and there familiar—frequently no ideas at all. Schumann, Chopin, Berlioz, Liszt, the leaders of the revolutionary movement in music after Beethoven (in which period Schumann indeed expected a Messiah and thought he had found him in—Brahms) have passed by our symphonist without leaving a trace on him; he was, or pretended to be, blind when the eyes of astonished mankind were opened by the dazzling genius of Wagner.... Just as people at that time danced minuets, i.e., wrote symphonies, so Herr Brahms also writes symphonies regardless of what has happened in the meantime. He is like a departed spirit that returns to its old house, totters up the rickety steps, turns the rusty key with much difficulty, and directs an absent-minded gaze on the cobwebs that are forming in the air and the ivy that is forcing its way through the gloomy windows.[152]

TCHAIKOVSKY and Brahms met on occasion and were cordial to one another. But Tchaikovsky could not abide Brahms the composer and said that while he revered Brahms's artistic purpose and recognized the purity of his artistic tendencies and his renunciation of all tricks, he did not care for his music.[153] Brahms's First Symphony had no charms for him; he found his music cold, obscure, pretentious, and without real depth. He also wrote in a letter to Nadejda von Meck that from the Russian point of view Brahms lacked melodic invention, and that the dry, cold, vague, and nebulous elements in his music were repellent to Russian hearts.[154]

SARASATE'S hyperbole about Brahms's Violin Concerto, in his riposte to Lalo, would not be shared by most violinists today: "Do you think me so devoid of taste that I would stand there in front of the orchestra, violin in hand, but like a listener, while the oboe plays the only melody in the entire work?"[155]

MAHLER too had his reservations about Brahms and compared him unfavorably to Wagner. He once wrote to his wife, Alma, that Brahms was a "puny little dwarf," and that if a breath from Wagner whistled about his ears he would scarcely be able to keep on his feet. He also remarked that although Brahms's themes were beautiful, he could very seldom make anything of them.[156] Mahler believed that Brahms was unable to free himself from the bonds of the grief and life of this earth and soar in freer and more radiant spheres; he always remained imprisoned in this world and could never attain the view from the peak. "His works can never, and will never, exercise the highest, ultimate influence."[157] Nonetheless Mahler admired Brahms's mastery of the variation form, writing about the *Variations on the St. Antony Chorale*: "Brahms's Variations are like an enchanted stream, with banks so sure that its waters never overflow, even in sharpest bends."[158]

RAVEL perceived a weakness in Brahms, coming as he did after Beethoven:

> This is what appears most clearly in the majority of Brahms's works. . . . [In the Symphony No. 2] the themes bespeak an intimate and gentle musicality; although their melodic contour and rhythm are very personal, they are directly related to those of Schubert and Schumann. Scarcely have they been presented when their progress becomes heavy and laborious. It seems that the composer had been ceaselessly haunted by the desire to equal Beethoven.[159]

Of more recent composers, BRITTEN did not have an unqualified admiration for Brahms. He said that Brahms was a major passion until he was seventeen, "then I suddenly found that his music didn't contain what I needed at that moment. I love the early works still—the D Minor Concerto and the Piano Quintet. In striving for formal perfection, I feel he somehow lost something, and that something is what I miss in his later music."[160]

POULENC said: "Brahms had the defects of Schumann without his genius. Admittedly he had his own, but it is a genius that leaves me totally indifferent."[161] STRAVINSKY, however, had a warm admiration for Brahms, and we give him the last word:

> I have a great feeling for Brahms. You always sense the overpowering wisdom of this great artist even in his least inspired works. . . . What the public likes in Brahms is the sentiment. What I like is another, the architectural basis.[162]

Benjamin Britten
(1913–1976)

Britten's fellow British composer, TIPPETT, wrote in his obituary for him:

> Britten has been for me the most purely musical person I have ever met
> and I have ever known. It always seemed to me that music sprang out of
> his fingers when he played the piano, as it did out of his mind when he
> composed.[163]

SHOSTAKOVICH dedicated his Fourteenth Symphony to Britten, and
was quoted as saying that he considered Britten to be then the greatest
living composer. Shostakovich also regarded the *War Requiem* as the greatest work of the twentieth century.[164] Britten himself acknowledged his debt
to Shostakovich's Fifth Symphony, as well as in his *Variations on a Theme
of Frank Bridge* and the *Sinfonia da Requiem*.

STRAVINSKY spoke very little of Britten; he once remarked about *A
Midsummer Night's Dream*: "It is a mistake to conclude each act with
people going to sleep."[165]

Max Bruch
(1838–1920)

Bruch is said to have asked BRAHMS to be allowed to play to him his first violin concerto from the manuscript. Brahms consented and seated himself near the piano. When Bruch had finished, Brahms rose, took a sheet of the manuscript between his thumb and middle finger, and, rubbing it between them, said: "I say, where do you buy your music paper? First rate!"[166]

Anton Bruckner
(1824–1896)

Bruckner was closely associated with Wagner in the schism that occurred in the nineteenth century when the followers of Wagner and Brahms were divided into separate camps. Richard Specht recorded a conversation he had with BRAHMS in the year of the latter's death in which he said:

> [Bruckner's] devout faith struck him as priest-ridden bigotry and he rated his vast symphonic structures as the amateurish, confused and illogical abortions of a crafty rustic schoolmaster. . . . What he said to me, approximately, was this: "Bruckner? That is a swindle which will be forgotten a year or two after my death. Take it as you will, Bruckner owes his fame solely to me, and but for me nobody would have cared a brass farthing for him. Do you really believe that anyone in this immature crowd has the least notion what these symphonic boa-constrictors are about? . . . And Bruckner's works immortal, and 'symphonies'? It is ludicrous!"[167]

On the other hand, WEINGARTNER tells in his memoirs that when he talked to Brahms about Bruckner, "Brahms listened quite calmly and spoke of Bruckner with respect, but without warmth."[168]

Bruckner visited WAGNER in 1873, and Wagner said after the meeting: "I know only one composer who approaches Beethoven—and that is Bruckner."[169] Bruckner dedicated his Third Symphony to Wagner; the circumstances in which he did this, during the visit of 1873, were:

> Of the three scores Bruckner brought with him, Wagner chose that of the Third Symphony, and summoned the delighted Bruckner to his new villa where the dedication was celebrated with tankards of beer. So intoxicated did Bruckner become with a mixture of beer and exultation that the next

day he could not remember for sure which symphony Wagner had accepted, and had to write to him to confirm that it was indeed the No. 3
in D Minor—"the one where the trumpet begins the theme," as he described it.[170]

As one of the Wagner camp, WOLF often wrote of Bruckner's music
in the highest terms. However, he could regard the composer with de-
tachment and is quoted as saying: "It is a deficiency on the intellectual
side, notwithstanding all their originality, greatness, imagination and inventiveness that makes the Bruckner symphonies so hard to understand.
Everywhere a will, a colossal purpose, but no satisfaction, no artistic so-
lution."[171]

MAHLER, too, did not accept Bruckner unreservedly, saying that while
one is carried away by the magnificence and wealth of his inventiveness,
its fragmentary character was frequently disturbing and broke the spell.[172]
Mahler also said about the Fourth Symphony: "One really cannot expect
the public to listen to musical junk and the worst kind of absurdities, even
though they may frequently contain divine ideas and themes."[173] But Alma
Mahler, Gustav's wife, wrote that in the title page of his copy of Bruckner's
Te Deum Mahler had crossed out the words "For chorus, soli and orchestra,
organ ad libitum" and written "For the tongues of angels, heaven-blest,
chastened hearts, and souls purified in fire!"[174]

Ferruccio Busoni
(1866–1924)

GRAINGER, the Australian composer and pianist, who was a pupil of Busoni, said:

> Busoni got brilliant results with next to no effort. I was slow and peg-away. Busoni impressed people immensely, but pleased few. I was able to please almost everybody including Busoni, but impressed nobody. Busoni was a big town artist, I a small town artist. My patience and humble stamina must have been just as annoying to Busoni as his flashy pretentiousness to me.[175]

KRENEK described to Stravinsky Busoni's soirées in Berlin shortly after the 1914–18 war, saying that the composer sat between a fortune-telling mystic and—for good luck, like Verdi's Duke of Mantua—a hunchback, and that this odd trinity was always separated from the guests by a row of empty chairs. "Busoni did all the talking, and he was seldom less than brilliant; he had great qualities of imagination, and great visionary powers—far beyond his abilities as a composer to realise his ideas."[176]

John Cage
(b. 1912)

COPLAND summed up the music of John Cage:

> How one reacts to Cage's ideas seems to me largely to depend on one's own personal temperament. Those who envisage art as a bulwark against the irrationality of man's nature, and as a monument to his constructive powers, will have no part of the Cagean aesthetic. But those who enjoy teetering on the edge of chaos will clearly be attracted.[177]

Emmanuel Chabrier
(1841–1894)

RAVEL was a great admirer of the music of Chabrier, although we have
no direct quotation from him beyond an acknowledgment of Chabrier's
influence on him. LAMBERT, the English conductor, composer, and
critic, wrote in his book *Music Ho!*:

> Chabrier holds one's affection as the most genuinely French of all com-
> posers, the only writer to give us in music the genial rich humanity, the
> inspired commonplace, the sunlit solidity of the French genius that finds
> its greatest expression in the paintings of Manet and Renoir.[178]

Carlos Chávez
(1899–1978)

Writing at the time when Chávez was twenty-eight years of age, COP-
LAND said:

> Chávez is essentially of our own day because he uses his composer's gift
> for the expression of objective beauty of universal significance rather than
> as a mere means of self-expression. Composing to him is a natural function,
> like eating or sleeping. His music is not a substitute for living but a
> manifestation of life. It exemplifies the complete overthrow of nineteenth-
> century Germanic ideals which tyrannized over music for more than a
> hundred years. It propounds no problems, no metaphysics. Chávez' music
> is extraordinarily healthy; it is clear and clean-sounding, without shadows
> or softness. Here is absolute music if ever there was any.[179]

Luigi Cherubini
(1760–1842)

We have only one short quotation about Cherubini, but it is an important one. BEETHOVEN, his contemporary, was once asked: "Who is the greatest living composer, yourself excepted?" He seemed puzzled for a moment, then exclaimed "Cherubini."[180]

Frédéric Chopin
(1810–1849)

SCHUMANN was perhaps the first to recognize Chopin when he wrote his famous article in 1831 in *Allgemeine Musikalische Zeitung* after he had seen Chopin's *Variations in B Flat on Là ci darem*, Op. 2. His words included the famous phrase, "Off with your hats, gentlemen—a genius!" Schumann was disappointed with Chopin's subsequent music, perceiving only a basic sameness of style—in a word, "mannered."[181]

LISZT wrote perceptively about Chopin:

> Chopin will have to be classed among the first musicians who have ... individualized in their own work the poetic feeling of a whole nation. . . . Pre-eminently a subjective composer, Chopin has given to all his creations the same life, and it is his own life which animates all his works. They are bound together in a unity which determines at once their beauties and their defects: both are the consequence of a single order of emotion, of an exclusive way of feeling—which indeed is essential if a poet is to cause the hearts of all his compatriots to beat as one.[182]

MENDELSSOHN was not sympathetic to Chopin's music, as he says in a letter to Moscheles: "A book of mazurkas by Chopin and a few new pieces of his are so mannered that they are hard to stand." But he admired him as a pianist: "There is something so thoroughly original and at the same time so very masterly in his piano playing that he may be called a really perfect virtuoso. I was glad to be once again with a thorough musician . . . one who has his own perfect and clearly defined style."[183]

BIZET wrote: "Only one man has been able to do quasi-improvised music, or what seems like it, and that is Chopin. . . . His personality is charming, strange, unique, and one should not try to imitate him."[184] To RAVEL, Chopin was a god, reported the French pianist Gaby Casadesus. She added: "Ravel used to say of the *Tarantella*, which is usually thought to be a cheap piece of Chopin, 'You ought to play it, not just for the Tarantella itself but for the beautiful chord at the end.'"[185] MESSIAEN too admires Chopin: "I love Chopin *qua* pianist-composer and also *qua* colorist, for, in my view, he's a very great colorist. Because he only wrote for the piano, why should he be put in a little box?"[186]

Russian composers were somewhat more critical. PROKOFIEV said: "Chopin's concertos struck me as being not so much concertos as piano pieces to which the orchestra has been added. I adored his E Minor theme, but one could get along very nicely without an orchestral accompaniment for it."[187] And STRAVINSKY: "Beautiful, but not for me."[188]

Muzio Clementi (1752–1832)

Although Clementi did not hesitate to declare his admiration for Mozart's genius, MOZART himself was always critical of Clementi. Clementi wrote over sixty sonatas, which Mozart disparaged in a letter to his father:

> Well, I have a few words to say to my sister about Clementi's sonatas. Everyone who either hears them or plays them must feel that as compositions they are worthless. They contain no remarkable or striking passages except those in sixths and octaves. And I implore my sister not to practise these passages too much, so that she may not spoil her quiet, even touch and that her hand may not lose its natural lightness, flexibility and smooth rapidity. . . . What he really does well are his passages in thirds; but he sweated over them day and night in London. Apart from this, he can do nothing, absolutely nothing, for he has not the slightest expression or taste, still less, feeling.[189]

Aaron Copland
(b. 1900)

Copland is now a father figure in American music, and although his compositions are in an essentially conservative (i.e., tonal) style, his early work was arresting. STRAVINSKY said that the *Dance Symphony* was "a very precocious opus for a composer of twenty-three."[190] VIRGIL THOMSON wrote this of Copland: "We have . . . a national glory in the form of Aaron Copland, who so skilfully combines, in the Bartók manner, folk feeling with neo-Classical techniques that foreigners often fail to recognise his music as American at all."[191]

Claude Debussy
(1862–1918)

In the public mind Debussy is coupled with Ravel, and it was RAVEL who said, when asked what music he would select if he were preparing a musical program for his own funeral: "*L'Après-midi d'un faune* . . . because it's the only score ever written that's absolutely perfect."[192] On another occasion Ravel said: "*La Mer* is poorly orchestrated. If I had the time, I would re-orchestrate *La Mer*."[193] At the same time he also made this observation about Debussy's orchestration: "One cannot say that his music is badly orchestrated, but it's written in such a way that nobody is able to learn anything from it. Only Debussy could have written it and made it sound like only Debussy can sound."[194] Ravel also commented about Debussy's use of form:

> Debussy had shown a *négligence de la forme*; he achieved through intellectual perception what Chopin had done from inspiration or intuition. Thus, in the larger forms, he showed a lack of architectural power. In a masterpiece like *L'Après-midi d'un faune*, where he achieved perfection, it was impossible to say how it had been built up.[195]

KODÁLY also wrote about this aspect of Debussy's music: "Even in his most intentionally formless music . . . some Latin heritage saves him from formlessness."[196] In his obituary for Debussy after the latter's death in 1918, Kodály wrote that even at the time of his death Debussy was still developing, that he was undoubtedly the most distinguished musician of his generation, and that his influence was most productive. He saw that his legacy may prove to be the inspiration he gave, rather than what he actually believed. "In his music he sought to portray . . . the most transient moods, to express the unfolding of an emotion, to trace precisely the fluctuations of the spirit." The extent of his world was not comparable to those of the few truly great musicians, "but within his own world he is a poet, and more than this no man can be."[197]

Shortly after Debussy's death, PUCCINI wrote in a letter:

> Claude Debussy had the soul of an artist shot through with a genuine and subtle sensibility. . . . His harmonic procedures which, when they were first made known, appeared so surprising and full of new beauty, became less and less so in the course of time until ultimately they surprised no one.[198]

SAINT-SAËNS was antipathetic to Debussy and his music. He wrote in a letter:

> The *Prélude à l'après-midi d'un faune* has pretty sonority, but one does not find in it the least musical idea, properly speaking; it resembles a piece of music as the palette used by an artist in his work resembles a picture. Debussy did not create a style; he cultivated an absence of style, logic, and common sense.[199]

But Sacha Guitry, the great actor, slyly observed that "if Monsieur Camille Saint-Saëns was determinedly wedded to Glory, I have a notion that she deceived him with Debussy."[200]

These verses by SATIE were published posthumously; they were titled "The Commandments of the Conservatory Catechism":

I. Thou shalt adore God-Debussy only,
   And copy him perfectly.

II. Thou shalt never be melodious
   In fact or by condonement.

III. Thou shalt abstain from planning ever,
   So as to compose with more facility.

IV. With great care thou shalt violate
   The rules of the old primer.

V. Thou shalt use consecutive fifths
   As well as consecutive octaves.

VI. Thou shalt never—oh never—
   Resolve a dissonance in any manner.

VII. Thou shalt never end a piece
With a consonant chord.

VIII. Thou shalt accumulate ninth-chords
Without any discrimination.

 IX. Thou shalt not desire a perfect concord
Except in marriage.

Ad Gloriam Tuam.[201]

RIMSKY-KORSAKOV attended a concert with Stravinsky at which one of Debussy's works was being played. Stravinsky asked him what he thought of it, and he replied: "Better not listen to him; one runs the risk of getting accustomed to him and one would end by liking him."[202] But STRAVINSKY himself named Debussy's *Études* as his favorite opus in the music of this century.[203]

DELIUS was not so impressed by Debussy:

> "Cleverness" counts for very little in my opinion. The younger French composers are all far too clever. Debussy wrote his best things before he was thirty, and gradually got more superficial and uninteresting. His best work is *L'Après-midi*, parts of *Pelléas* are very fine and there is great dignity in the work. These I consider works that will live, but none of the others.[204]

BARTÓK compared Debussy to Bach and Beethoven:

> Debussy's great service to music was to reawaken among all musicians an awareness of harmony and its possibilities. In that, he was just as important as Beethoven, who revealed to us the meaning of progressive form, and as Bach, who showed us the transcendant significance of counterpoint.[205]

MESSIAEN was asked which composers, in his view, were largely responsible for the speedy evolutionary progress of modern music. He replied: "In the very first place, Debussy, who introduced the idea of haziness, not only in harmony and melody but above all in rhythm and in the succession of timbres. After him came Schoenberg."[206]

BOULEZ regarded Debussy as the only French composer who is universal in the last two centuries. He wrote that Debussy's life was a quest for a development that incorporated surprises arising from the imagination; he distrusted architecture and preferred structures that combined rigor and freedom of choice. "The habitual mental categories of a worn-out tradition could never be applied to his works, even if we tried to adjust them by twisting them here and there."[207]

COPLAND wrote: "Debussy, one of the most instinctive musicians who ever lived, was the first composer of our time who dared to make his ear the sole judge of what was good harmonically."[208]

D'INDY'S assessment of *Pelléas et Mélisande* was:

> *Pelléas*, obviously, is neither an opera nor a lyric drama . . . it is both less and more: less, because music *per se* plays in it, most of the time, only a subordinate part—a part comparable to that of the illuminations in medieval manuscripts, or of polychromy in medieval sculpture; and more, because here is the text that stands essential—the text whose musical setting constitutes a wonderful adaptation, bringing color to the design, revealing the hidden meaning of the words, and intensifying their expressive power.[209]

LAMBERT, writing in *Music Ho!*, had a much lesser view of Debussy's opera, writing that it is one of his weakest and most mannered works and represented a phase that Debussy had to go through before he could rid himself completely of the oppressive weight of the Teutonic Romantic tradition.[210] On the other hand, *La Mer*, in Lambert's estimation, was the most finished and typical of Debussy's compositions. It represents the apex of his impressionist manner in its abandonment of formal principle, in its absence of a continuous melodic line and of development in the accepted sense of the word, and in the pointillism of its scoring.[211]

FAURÉ was asked after he had heard the orchestra rehearse the movement *De l'aube à midi sur la mer* whether he liked the music. He replied: "Indeed, especially the little bit at thirteen minutes to twelve."[212]

Finally, from BLOCH, who lamented Debussy's fate:

> The fate of Debussy has been the usual one. First, he was ignored. Now he is understood and admired only through his superficial and trivial qualities. An army of imitators, of second-hand manufacturers, pounced on the technique of Claude Debussy. . . . The language of Debussy has become vulgarized and denatured; false image has emptied it of its native color. It has become a mechanical procedure, without power and without soul.[213]

Frederick Delius
(1862–1934)

Born in England of German descent, Delius settled in France in 1899, where he lived for the rest of his life. Nonetheless he is regarded as a British composer, especially by the French; NADIA BOULANGER, the French composer, teacher, and conductor, said that there was in Delius "something which the French could never recognise as their own."[214] Yet VAUGHAN WILLIAMS observed, with Delius's composition *Brigg Fair* in mind:

> The more level-headed of us do not imagine that because Delius used an English folksong in one of his compositions it makes him into an Englishman. Those who claim England as the birthplace of Delius's art must base their arguments on more valid premises than this.[215]

BAX had much in common with Delius and explained it thus:

> I am absolutely certain that the only music that can last is that which is the outcome of one's emotional reactions to the ultimate realities of Life, Love and Death. . . . I believe in conditions of ecstasy—physical or spiritual—and I get nothing from anything else. I think all the composers who appeal to me—Beethoven, Wagner, Delius, Sibelius—were primitive in that they believed that the secret of the universe could be solved by ecstatic intuition rather than by thought. All our unrest and melancholy is caused by conscience and remorse inhibiting nature. I do believe that all original ideas derive from some condition of untrammelled passion and ecstasy.[216]

LAMBERT wrote in 1934 that "the music of today seems either to be a romantic swan song regretting past days, as in Delius, an alembicated and intellectual crossword puzzle, as in von Webern, or a callow reflection of the drab minutiae of daily life, as in Hindemith."[217] GRAINGER knew Delius well, admired his music, and more than once pointed out that Delius was essentially a composesr who wrote music expressing the moods of nature: [Delius was] the first superlative genius amongst the 'nature music' composers. As such he naturally excels in the musical depiction of those moods that invariably accompany the 'nature emotions': loneliness, wistfulness, frailness, dreaminess, turned-inwardness, vagueness, and a sense of distance."[218]

DUKE ELLINGTON was once told by Grainger that his jazz music had striking resemblances to the music of Delius. Ellington was greatly puzzled because he had never heard Delius's name, let alone his music. Not being a man of narrow culture, Ellington bought all the available records of Delius and had many of the English Columbia records by Beecham imported. He listened to them all with intense interest. Although this made him a lifelong lover of the music of Delius, it did not convince him of any similarity such as Grainger had suggested.[219]

Antonín Dvořák
(1841–1904)

The French conductor and composer PIERNÉ was the center of a controversy in Paris shortly after World War I concerning Dvořák's Cello Concerto. Pablo Casals, the eminent cellist, came to Paris once a year to perform at the benefit concert for the Lamoureux and Colonne orchestras. Pierné was the chief conductor of the Colonne Orchestra and had arranged with Casals beforehand that Casals should play the Dvořák concerto. After Casals arrived in Paris for the concert, he met Pierné just prior to the dress rehearsal, which an audience attended, to decide tempi and other details of the performance. While they were discussing the score, Pierné suddenly threw it onto the table and exclaimed, "What horrible music!" Casals believed Pierné was joking and asked him what he meant. Pierné repeated what he had said. Casals retorted: "Are you mad? How can you insult such a magnificent work?" Pierné replied that as a musician Casals must know how bad the music was. Casals became very upset, protesting that if Pierné scorned and detested the work, it was obvious that he did not understand it, and that he could not possibly interpret it. Casals then added that the situation was impossible and that he would not play.

The audience was filling the hall, and the news that Casals would not be playing caused a furor. Casals saw Debussy standing by and said to him: "Ask [Pierné] if he thinks an artist can possibly play when feeling as I do." Debussy's reply astonished and pained Casals: "Come on," said Debussy, "if you wanted to play, you would play." He replied to Debussy: "I assure you it is impossible for me to play and I will not play." Casals prepared to leave, but Pierné ordered a bailiff to serve Casals with a summons. When the subsequent law case came to trial, the judge pronounced against Casals, and he had to pay damages and court costs. However, Pierné's attorney conceded in court that Casals had artistic justification for his behavior.[220]

BRAHMS exercised considerable influence over Dvořák and gave him much encouragement and assistance. Dvořák once replied to a letter from Brahms:

> I have read your last most cherished letter with the most joyful excitement; your warm encouragement and the pleasure you seem to find in my work, have moved me deeply and made me happy beyond expression. I can hardly tell you, dear master, all that is in my heart. I can only say that I shall all my life owe you the deepest gratitude for your good and noble intentions towards me, which are worthy of a truly great artist and man.[221]

Brahms was so impressed by Dvořák's *Moravian Duets* that he wrote to the publisher Simrock urging him to accept them. But Dvořák was astonished at Brahms's lack of religious faith, saying: "Such a great man! Such a great soul! And he believes in nothing!"[222] Brahm's reaction when he first read the score of Dvořák's Cello Concerto was to ask himself: "Why on earth didn't I know that one could write a violoncello concerto like this? If I had only known, I would have written one long ago."[223]

Sir Edward Elgar
(1857–1934)

Elgar's music has, until recent times, been infrequently performed outside of England. Yet it was in Düsseldorf, Germany, that his great oratorio *The Dream of Gerontius* was first acclaimed. Elgar was self-taught as a composer; PADEREWSKI, the Polish pianist, composer, and statesman, was asked where Elgar studied. "Nowhere!" "Then who taught him?" "Le Bon Dieu!"[224]

Two contemporary British composers made these comments.
BLISS:

> Elgar was a man, I consider, of inspired musical personality. He wrote because he was compelled to do so. . . . I think he was a very sensitive, highly imaginative, often harassed human being, and whenever I hear the slow movement from the First Symphony I see the man: especially do I see a clear-cut image of him in the final bars.[225]

WALTON:

> His symphonies are much better than those of Mahler and Bruckner.[226]

DELIUS met Elgar, who said to him: "My music will not interest you, Delius; you are too much of a poet for a workman like me!" Delius replied that he thought there was some fine stuff in his Introduction and Allegro for strings, and that he admired his *Falstaff,* but he thought it was a great pity that he had wasted so much time and energy in writing those long-winded oratorios. "That," said Elgar, "is the penalty of my English environment."[227] On another occasion Delius said:

I find Elgar's musical invention weak; whenever he gets hold of a good theme or nice harmonies they remind me of *Parsifal* or Brahms. He never seems to have outlived his admiration for the Good Friday Music; he has it also in *Gerontius*. His manner of composition is also Brahms's. And then the Symphony [No. 1] is very long, and the orchestration thick and clumsy, as is also Brahms's. I heard the Violin Concerto in London, and I find it long and dull.[228]

RICHARD STRAUSS was a friend and admirer of Elgar. The day after the Düsseldorf performance of *The Dream of Gerontius* on 20 May 1902, Strauss proposed a toast to "the first English progressivist, Meister Edward Elgar."[229]

For an American view on Elgar, let VIRGIL THOMSON speak:

Like most English composers, Elgar orchestrates accurately and competently. . . . I've an idea the Elgar [*Enigma*] Variations are mostly a pretext for orchestration, a pretty pretext and a graceful one, but a pretext for fancywork all the same, for that massively frivolous patchwork in pastel shades of which one sees such qualities in any intellectual British suburban dwelling.[230]

César Franck
(1812–1890)

Opinion was divided about Franck among his fellow contemporary French composers—if one may be forgiven for so describing one who was born in Belgium but lived most of his life in France. D'INDY, who was a pupil, follower, and biographer of Franck, had the highest opinion of him, asking where there would be another composer in the second half of the nineteenth century who was capable of thinking as loftily as Franck, or who "could have found in his fervent and enthusiastic heart such vast ideas" as those that are the musical bases of the Quartet, the Symphony or the oratorio *Les Béatitudes.* Franck's Symphony, wrote d'Indy, "is a continual ascent towards pure gladness and life-giving light" and "its themes are manifestations of ideal beauty." D'Indy also referred to the mystical significance of *Psyché,* which, he said, "has nothing of the pagan spirit about it," but "is imbued with Christian grace and feeling."[231]

DUKAS said that Franck's musical language was quite individual, completely new and recognizable. It was possible to recognize any of his musical phrases, even if one had not heard them before. His harmony and melodic style are as distinctive as those of Chopin and Wagner. For Dukas, Franck's music owes its greatness to "powerful musical originality . . . the breadth of expression . . . manifested in traditional forms with a vocabulary and syntax hitherto unknown."[232]

RAVEL wrote of the Symphony: "Melody of a cultivated and cheerful spirit, daring harmonies of especial richness, but a devastating poverty of form."[233] SAINT-SAËNS is quoted as having said this about Franck's Prelude, Chorale, and Fugue:

A piece ungraceful and awkward to play, in which the Chorale is not a chorale and the Fugue is not a fugue, for as soon as the exposition is over it loses heart and perpetuates itself in never-ending digressions which no more resemble a fugue than a zoophyte [low-level organism] resembles a mammifer [mammal], thus exacting a heavy toll for the brilliant peroration.[234]

DELIUS was more charitable:

I think a good deal of Franck. The Symphony and the Sonata I consider the works which will live. . . . I like the first movement of the Sonata and some of the Symphony, and that is all. I never find him quite original, and influenced greatly by Wagner, Schumann and Grieg.[235]

George Gershwin
(1898–1937)

BERNSTEIN was an admirer of Gershwin and frequently performed the *Rhapsody in Blue*. However, he has a poor opinion of Gershwin's competence as a composer, as opposed to a songwriter:

> The *Rhapsody [in Blue]* is not a composition at all. It's a string of separate paragraphs stuck together—with a thin paste of flour and water. Composing is a very different thing from writing tunes, after all. I find that the themes, or tunes, or whatever you call them, in the *Rhapsody* are terrific—inspired, God-given. . . . I don't think there has been such an inspired melodist on this earth since Tchaikovsky. . . . But if you want to speak of a *composer*, that is another matter. Your *Rhapsody in Blue* is not a real composition in the sense that whatever happens in it must seem inevitable, or even pretty inevitable.[236]

Bernstein wrote also about *An American in Paris* in the same article:

> When you hear this piece, you rejoice in the first theme, then sit and wait through the "filler" until the next one comes along. In this way you sit out two-thirds of the composition. The remaining third is marvellous because it consists of the themes themselves; but where's the composition?[237]

Stories have circulated about Gershwin and RAVEL, STRAVINSKY, and SCHOENBERG. In fact, Gershwin was a near neighbor of Schoenberg when they both lived in Brentwood in Los Angeles, and the two regularly played tennis on the court at Gershwin's house. It is said that Gershwin asked Schoenberg to take him on as a pupil; Schoenberg refused, saying:

"I would only make you a bad Schoenberg and you're such a good Gershwin already!" Another story is repeated about Gershwin asking RAVEL, or was it Stravinsky, for lessons. Ravel (or Stravinsky) asked: "How much do you earn a year from your compositions?" "Around $100,000," replied Gershwin. "In that case, you give *me* lessons."[238]

Alexander Glazunov
(1865–1936)

SHOSTAKOVICH was a student of Glazunov at the Leningrad Conservatory, and in his memoirs there are many comments about the man and his music. This is one:

> Glazunov is a marvellous example of a purely Russian phenomenon: as a composer he can honestly and fairly hold a position in the history of Russian music that is not simply outstanding but unique, and not only because of his compositions.... I suppose I value his Eighth Symphony more than the others, particularly the slow movement. The others contain rather flabby music. Boring actually.[239]

STRAVINSKY dismissed Glazunov's music as "academic," by that meaning that it was shapeless and unformed, although he admitted Glazunov's contribution to the world of academic music.[240]

According to M. D. Calvocoressi,

> [RAVEL] belonged to the number of the few who held Glazunov's early works in high esteem—especially the tone poems *The Forest, Stenka Razin,* the *Oriental Rhapsody,* and the second and third symphonies. Of course we were not blind to their derivative character; yet we felt that Glazunov displayed strong personality and fine imagination.[241]

Mikhail Glinka
(1804–1857)

Described as the "father of Russian music," Glinka wrote the first really national opera, *Russlan and Ludmilla.* TCHAIKOVSKY said of him: "There is a genuine Russian symphonic school. It is all in [Glinka's] *Kamarinskaya,* just as an oak tree is in an acorn."[242] Tchaikovsky also said of *A Night in Madrid* by Glinka:

> How much warm inspiration and luxurious poetic fantasy there is in this fascinating composition of our great artist! The extraordinary original overture describing the transparent twilight of the approaching southern night; the passionately captivating sounds of the dance band heard in the distance; the quickly changing episodes in the middle section in which is heard a mysterious prattle, a kiss, an embrace, and then, again, a calm under the cover of a fragrant, starry, southern night.[243]

BERLIOZ wrote that "Glinka has the right to occupy a place alongside the outstanding composers of his time."[244]

Christoph Gluck
(1714–1787)

The feelings of Mozart, Haydn, and Beethoven towards Gluck are not at all clear beyond the fact that they held him in the greatest respect. We know that Beethoven played on the piano the score of *Iphigénie en Tauride* while a group of French generals and officers, obviously very musical, sang the arias and choruses when they visited him in Vienna in 1805. SALIERI referred to Gluck in a letter to the Empress Marie Antoinette as "that sublime genius, the creator of dramatic music, which he has carried to the highest degree of perfection it is capable of attaining."[245]

BERLIOZ worshipped Gluck and wrote that when he was a student, Gluck was "the Jove of our Olympus." He said that if some of his colleagues were zealous adherents of the faith in their worship of Gluck, he was the high priest.[246]

VERDI had his reservations: "I can't help feeling that despite his great dramatic temperament [Gluck] was not far superior to the greatest of his day, and as a musician he was inferior to Handel."[247]

When he produced Gluck's *Iphigénie en Aulide* in Dresden in 1847, WAGNER carried out a revision of the score, writing in his autobiography that he "tried to bring the poem as far as possible into agreement with Euripides' play of the same name." He goes on:

> For the sake of the vitality of the drama I tried to join the arias and the choruses, which generally followed immediately upon each other without rhyme or reason, by connecting links, prologues and epilogues. In this I did my best, by the use of Gluck's themes, to make the interpolations of a strange composer as unnoticeable as possible. . . . I revised the whole

instrumentation more or less thoroughly, but only with the object of making the existing version produce the effect I desired.[248]

One wonders what Wagner's reaction would be if later composers rewrote his operas with the same nonchalance.

Carl Goldmark
(1830–1915)

When MAHLER was in Hamburg, he and Brahms went together to hear Goldmark's *Sakuntala* Overture. Mahler said that both were irritated by the music and came away agreeing that Goldmark's music was superficial. But Mahler thought the exception was the opera *Die Königin von Saba* (The Queen of Sheba), saying "The first two acts enchant me, especially the scene in the temple. The music of the Ark of the Covenant is really great, there is something of the Old Testament in its power and splendour."[249]

Charles Gounod
(1818–1893)

VERDI was an admirer of Gounod, but with some reservations, saying that while "Gounod's is a refined and charming talent, his *Faust* is a first-rate work, although it is not a true representation of Goethe, as is Boito's *Mefistofele*."[250] He said also that although Gounod wrote excellent chamber and instrumental music, he was not an artist of dramatic fibre. *Faust*, while a successful opera, became small in his hands, as his treatment of situations was weak and his characterization was poor.[251]

BIZET said about *Faust*: "I am convinced that the tenor's role is badly written for the voice. But I am also convinced that *Faust* is a master-piece."[252] RAVEL also defended Gounod; Calvocoressi wrote that at a time when Gounod's music used to be sneered at in "advanced" circles, Ravel passionately called attention to the lovely things to be found in it.[253] Ravel also wrote: "Gounod, the true originator of melody in France, Gounod, who rediscovered the secret of a harmonic sensuousness lost since the harpsichordists of the XVIIth and XVIIIth centuries."[254]

Edvard Grieg
(1843–1907)

DELIUS once said that Grieg's music "at its best is so fresh, poetic and original, just like Norway."[255] DEBUSSY, who wrote facetiously about many of his contemporary composers and offended Grieg with one of his writings in the Parisian journal *Gil Blas,* described his music as "bonbons stuffed with snow."[256] TCHAIKOVSKY understood Grieg's special individuality:

> Grieg is probably not by any means as great a master as Brahms; his aims and tendencies are not so wide, and apparently in Grieg the inclination towards obscurity is entirely absent; nonetheless he stands nearer to us, he seems more approachable and intelligible because of his deep humanity. Hearing the music of Grieg we instinctively recognise that it was written by a man impelled by an irresistible impulse to give vent by means of sounds to a flood of poetic emotion, which obeys no theory or principle, is stamped with no impress but that of a vigorous and sincere artistic feeling. Perfection of form, strict and irreproachable logic in the development of his themes, are not perseveringly sought after by the celebrated Norwegian. But what charm, what inimitable and rich musical imagery! What warmth and passion in his melodic phrases, what teeming vitality in his harmony, what originality and beauty in the turn of his piquant and ingenious modulations and rhythms, and in all the rest what interest, novelty and independence! If we add to all this that rarest of qualities, a perfect simplicity, far removed from affectation and pretence to obscurity and far-fetched novelty, it is not surprising that everyone should delight in Grieg.[257]

George Frideric Handel (1685–1759)

When HAYDN visited England in 1791, he heard *Messiah* performed at a Handel Festival in Westminster Abbey, with the performers numbering up to 1,000. At the "Hallelujah Chorus" Haydn sobbed, exclaiming "He is master of us all."[258] On another occasion Haydn heard the chorus "The Nations Tremble" from *Joshua* and remarked that "he had long been acquainted with music, but never knew half its powers before he heard the chorus, as he was perfectly certain that only one inspired author ever did, or ever would, pen so sublime a composition."[259]

BEETHOVEN's admiration for Handel was unbounded. He was once asked, "Whom do you consider the greatest composer that ever lived?" His immediate reply was "Handel. To him I bow the knee," and he then bent one knee to the floor.[260] He is also reported to have said: "Handel is the greatest composer that ever lived. I would uncover my head, and kneel down at his tomb!"[261] On his deathbed Beethoven received from Johann Stumpff in London the forty-volume edition of Samuel Arnold's edition of Handel's works; according to Thayer, one day the boy attending on him was asked to hand the big books from the pianoforte where they rested to the bed. "I have long awaited them," said Beethoven, "for Handel is the greatest, the ablest composer that ever lived. I can still learn from him!"[262]

WAGNER attended a performance of *Messiah* at Exeter Hall in London with a chorus of 700 voices. He recorded in his autobiography:

> It is here that I came to understand the true spirit of English Protestantism. This accounts for the fact that an oratorio attracts the public far more than an opera. A further advantage is secured by the feeling among the

audience that an evening spent in listening to an oratorio may be regarded as a sort of service, and is almost as good as going to church. Every one in the audience holds a Handel piano score in the same way as one holds a prayer-book in church. These scores are sold at the box-office in shilling editions, and are followed most diligently—out of anxiety, it seemed to me, not to miss certain points solemnly enjoyed by the whole audience. For instance, at the beginning of the "Hallelujah" Chorus it is considered proper for everyone to rise from his seat. This movement, which probably originated in an expression of enthusiasm, is now carried out at each performance of the *Messiah* with painful precision.[263]

MENDELSSOHN wrote to his sister Fanny about Handel's *Coronation Anthem* (which one is not recorded): "It is most singular. The beginning is one of the finest which not only Handel, but any man ever composed; and all the remainder, after the short first movement, is horribly dry and commonplace."[264]

Much later SCHOENBERG made a similar criticism of Handel: "As a composer for the theatre Handel always had the power of beginning with a characteristic and often excellent theme. But, thereafter, with the exception of the repetitions of the theme there follows a decline bringing only . . . 'trash'—empty, meaningless, étude-like broken chord figures."[265] STRAVINSKY made the point another way: "Handel was the pop-tune, and the commercial composer. Bach was the inward one."[266]

Roy Harris
(1898–1979)

Writing in 1941, COPLAND said about Harris:

> The outstanding thing that sets Harris apart from other composers is the
> fact that he possesses one of the most pronounced musical personalities
> of anyone now writing. You can punch the personality full of holes—you
> can demonstrate to your own satisfaction that the man doesn't know the
> first thing about composing—but the fact will still remain that his is the
> most personal note in American music today. Moreover, it was there from
> the very start of his career. . . . Harris has grown in many ways. In fact,
> his capacity for growth has been astonishing.[267]

VIRGIL THOMSON remarked that Harris, "though the bearer of no
exceptional melodic gifts and the possessor of no really thorough musical
schooling, has an unquenchable passion to know and to use all the pro-
cedures of musical composition."[268] Later, in 1952, Thomson declared that
Harris's Third Symphony had "become America's most popular (and most
exportable) single expression in symphonic form."[269]

Franz Joseph Haydn
(1732–1809)

Haydn's close and most respected friend, MOZART, said of him:

> I learned from Haydn how to write quartets. No one else can do everything, jest and shock, create laughter and profound emotion, as Haydn can, and no one can do everything as well as Haydn can.[270]

Mozart dedicated his six string quartets K. 387, K. 421, K. 428, K. 458, K. 464, and K. 465 to Haydn, and in a letter to Haydn enclosing the quartets he wrote:

> During your last stay in this capital [Vienna] you yourself, my very dear friend, expressed to me your approval of these compositions. Your good opinion encourages me to offer them to you and leads me to hope that you will not consider them wholly unworthy of your favour. Please then receive them kindly and be to them a father, guide and friend! From this moment I surrender to you all my rights over them. I entreat you, however, to be indulgent to those faults which may have escaped a father's partial eye, and, in spite of them, to continue your generous friendship to one who so highly appreciates it. Meanwhile I remain with all my heart, dearest friend, your most sincere friend.[271]

On Haydn's seventy-sixth birthday in 1808 a performance of *The Creation* was given at the Vienna University. BEETHOVEN stood with the members of the nobility at the door to receive "the venerable guest on his arrival there in Prince Esterhazy's coach." Haydn was carried into the hall in an armchair to the sounds of trumpets and drums; Beethoven "knelt down before Haydn and fervently kissed the hands and forehead of his old teacher." After Haydn's death Beethoven always referred to him with the greatest praise and affection, regarding him as the equal of Handel, Bach, Gluck, and Mozart.[272]

SCHUMANN too had the highest opinion of Haydn:

> Heavenly harmony resides in [Haydn's] sounds, so free of traces of boredom, so productive of gaiety, zest for living [and] childlike joy.... What a service he has rendered, especially to the present age ... when men are so seldom inwardly satisfied.[273]

RICHARD STRAUSS said to aspiring composers who came to show him their "portentious symphonic poems": "Go home and study Haydn's symphonies and then the symphonies of Mozart, and come to me again in two years' time."[274] FURTWÄNGLER, the great German conductor, who also composed symphonies and a piano concerto, observed: "To my mind, Haydn is more of a symphonic composer than Mozart. The sense of the symphony is to be found in Haydn."[275] But IVES, the iconoclastic American composer, was rather less complimentary. He is reported to have sung along satirically after hearing Haydn's Symphony No. 94 (the *Surprise*) "*Pret*-ty *lit*-tle *sug*-ar *plum sounds*" and to have called it "easy music for the sissies."[276]

Hans Werner Henze
(b. 1926)

Two twentieth-century composers have opposing views about Henze. WALTON said in an interview in 1976:

> I think he's the only proper composer going today. I hate to say it, but it's no good mentioning Britten or Tippett or myself in the same breath as Hans. The only thing I've got against him is that he talks so much.[277]

But BOULEZ said, three years earlier:

> Whatever rubbish he puts out, he still believes he's king. A Beatles record is certainly cleverer than a Henze record, and shorter as well.[278]

Paul Hindemith
(1895–1963)

Geoffrey Skelton, in his biography of Hindemith, wrote:

> It is not surprising that Hindemith's critics should begin to wonder aloud
> if he were not merely a clever practitioner who could produce music by
> the yard under any sort of conditions. One of the sceptics was Richard
> Strauss . . . who asked Hindemith . . . how long he had taken to compose
> the work he had just heard. "Four days," Hindemith replied. Strauss
> remarked: "That's just what I thought!"[279]

But STRAUSS generally had no interest in the music of composers of
Hindemith's generation. He said to the young Hindemith once: "Why do
you compose like that? You don't need to—you have talent."[280]

SIBELIUS said about Hindemith: "First and foremost he is a German
artisan—very clever, but lacking in compulsion."[281] LAMBERT wrote that
Hindemith was able to deceive the ear by sheer quickness of hand, but
there was an absence of a genuine motive force or any genuine lyrical line
in his slow movements. He described his sense of form as not "an intrinsic
sense of form but an extrinsic use of formalism."[282]

VIRGIL THOMSON wrote in 1941:

> Paul Hindemith's music is both mountainous and mouselike. The volume
> of it is enormous; its expressive content is minute and not easy to catch.
> . . . How often has one sat through pieces by Hindemith that seem to make
> sense musically but little or no sense emotionally![283]

Arthur Honegger
(1892–1955)

After listening to an orchestral piece by Honegger, GERSHWIN said: "The European boys have small ideas but they sure know how to dress them up."[284] Writing about Honegger's *Pacific 231*, COPLAND stated: "*Pacific 231* is an excellent example of modern programme music; if it is not a great piece of music, it is because of the poor quality of some of the melodic material rather than the treatment of the programmatic idea itself."[285]

Charles Ives
(1874–1954)

After SCHOENBERG'S death in 1951, his widow sent Ives a note she had found among his papers. It read:

> There is a great man living in this country—a composer. He has solved the problem how to preserve one's self and to learn. He responds to negligence by contempt. He is not forced to accept praise or blame. His name is Ives.[286]

STRAVINSKY also recognized the greatness of Ives but pointed out that he was not a symphonist. *Three Places in New England*, he said, contains much better music than the Fourth Symphony and is more an entity than any of the symphonies. Nevertheless, the second movement of the Fourth Symphony is an "astonishing achievement."[287]

HERRMANN, the American composer and conductor, wrote of Ives in 1932:

> Mr. Ives puts cowboy tunes and hillbilly songs and camp-meeting hymns into his symphonies. These are the tunes of our country and we love them. ... We know that Mr. Ives belongs among the immortals and some day all the rest of America will know it. America will know it when it can appreciate the meaning of a new American tone, of a new dissonance. His music is our music. It is not European.[288]

Aram Khachaturian (1903–1978)

SHOSTAKOVICH wrote:

> Khachaturian's individuality—the result of his great creative gifts—reveals itself not only in his idiom, not only leaving his imprint on every bar; this individuality is broader and implies something more than musical technology alone: it comprises also the composer's outlook which is a basically optimistic, life-asserting view of our reality.... The national and folk idiom of his music is evident ... in all his compositions, however different their subject may be.[289]

Zoltán Kodály
(1882–1967)

His Hungarian compatriot and close colleague BARTÓK wrote of Kodály in 1921:

> Kodály is one of the most outstanding composers of our day. His art, like mine, has twin roots: it has sprung from Hungarian peasant music and modern French music. But though our art has grown from this common soil, our works from the very beginning have been completely different (It is sheer injustice or ignorance to declare that Kodály is an "imitator"). Some of his attackers continually reproach him for composing music that is less forceful, less original, and so forth than mine. . . . It is possible that [his] music is not so "aggressive"; it is possible that in form it is closer to certain traditions; it is possible that it expresses calm meditation rather than "unbridled orgies." But it is precisely this essential difference, reaching expression in his music as a completely new and original way of thinking, that makes his musical message so valuable.[290]

Édouard Lalo
(1823–1892)

TCHAIKOVSKY had a comment to make about the French composer Lalo: "In the same way as Delibes and Bizet, [Lalo] does not strive after profundity, but he carefully avoids routine, seeks out new forms, and thinks more about *musical beauty* than about observing established traditions, as do the Germans."[291]

D'INDY wrote that Lalo's Symphony in G Minor, "which is on very classical lines, is remarkable for the fascination of its themes, and still more for charm and elegance of rhythm and harmony, distinctive qualities of the imaginative composer of *Le Roi d'Ys*."[292]

Franz Lehár
(1870–1948)

In her memoirs Alma MAHLER related that she and her husband went to and enjoyed *The Merry Widow*. When they returned home they played the waltz from the operetta on the piano from memory and danced to it, but they could not remember exactly the run of one passage. Being too "highbrow," they could not face buying the music, so they went to Doblinger's music shop, and while Mahler was enquiring about the sale of his compositions, Alma casually turned the pages of the piano edition of *The Merry Widow* and located the passage she wanted. Once in the street she sang it, so that it would not slip her memory a second time.[293]

RACHMANINOV also enjoyed the operetta. In a letter from Dresden in 1907 he wrote: "I saw the operetta, *The Merry Widow*. Though written now, it too is a work of genius. I laughed like a fool. Absolutely wonderful."[294]

Franz Liszt
(1811–1886)

Liszt's contemporaries recognized the ambiguities in Liszt the man and the musician. SCHUMANN disapproved of Liszt's flamboyant manner of living, and doubted whether great music could result from it: "What may yet be expected from him is a matter of conjecture. To win the favor of his fatherland he would, above all things, have to return to serenity and simplicity."[295] He wrote to Clara Wieck:

> How extraordinarily he plays, boldly and wildly, and then again tenderly and ethereally! I have heard all this. But Clärchen, this world—his world I mean—is no longer mine. Art, as you practise it, and as I do when I compose at the piano, this tender intimacy I would not give for all his splendour—and indeed there is too much tinsel about it.[296]

Schumann also said about Liszt's piano arrangements of songs by Schubert: "A witty fellow wonders whether an easier arrangement could not be published, and also whether the result of one would be the original Schubert song again."[297]

WAGNER was close to Liszt, who was, after all, his father-in-law. Wagner studied Liszt's tone poems very closely, and they undoubtedly influenced him greatly. He wrote to Liszt on 20 July 1856:

> Your Symphonic Poems are now quite familiar to me; they are the only music which occupies me at present, for during my cure I must not think of doing any work. I read one or other of the scores every day, just as I might read a poem, fluently and without stopping. I feel every time as if I had dived into a deep crystal flood, to be there quite by myself, leaving all the world behind me, and living for an hour my real life.[298]

MENDELSSOHN was astonished when he showed Liszt the almost illegible manuscript of his piano concerto, and Liszt "played it at sight absolutely perfectly, better than anyone else could possibly play it—quite marvellously!" "A miracle—a *real* miracle," Mendelssohn exclaimed to Hiller.[299]

CHOPIN also admired Liszt the pianist, as he once wrote in a letter: "I write to you without knowing what I am scribbling, because Liszt is playing my studies and transporting me out of my respectable thoughts. I should like to steal from him his way of playing my own studies."[300]

TCHAIKOVSKY was not impressed when he attended the concert in honor of Liszt's seventieth birthday:

> Liszt's works leave me cold. They have more poetical intention than actual creative power, more color than form—in short, in spite of being externally effective, they are lacking in the deeper qualities. Liszt is just the opposite of Schumann, whose vast creative force is not in harmony with his colorless style of expression.[301]

RICHARD STRAUSS wrote ecstatically about Liszt on several occasions:

> Franz Liszt was the first creative genius of the nineteenth century, before Richard Wagner, to understand Beethoven correctly.[302]

> Liszt is the only symphonist, the only one who had to come after Beethoven and represents a gigantic advance upon him. Everthing else is drivel, pure and simple.[303]

> The lofty flight of the ideas and the deep inner emotion of the Purgatorio [in the *Dante* symphony]—the *Bénédiction*, a glorious, sublime piece— *Mazeppa*, a glorious piece, *Saint Elizabeth* is beautiful and deeply felt, so little handicraft and so much poetry, so little counterpoint and so much music. The first section of *Die Hunnenschlacht* is grandiose, the Mephisto waltz has an impudence that really only a genius can afford to indulge in—it has red blood and life.[304]

MAHLER scarcely agreed, criticizing the "meagre and shoddy workmanship of [Liszt's] compositions," which resembled a badly woven garment where the threads become visible soon after it has been worn.[305]

Liszt's fellow countryman, BARTÓK, considered that Liszt's influence on succeeding generations was more fertile than Wagner's.[306] No matter what he touched—Hungarian art song, folk song, Italian aria, or whatever—he so gave it his own individuality that it became unmistakably his music. More importantly, he mixed elements drawn from himself with these foreign sources in such a way that "there is no work in which we can doubt the greatness of his creative power."[307] Taking up Liszt's particular compositions, Bartók said that in the Piano Sonata, the subdued introductory bars, the pauses leading to the recitative-like music before the working-out section, the sombre coda, and the fugato, which is the greatest of all and "flashes with the very sparks of hell"—all these are among music's great things. The E Flat Piano Concerto is also perfect, the *Faust* Symphony is rendered immortal by its plenitude of wonderful thoughts, there is shattering music in the *Totentanz,* and the B-A-C-H Prelude and Fugue has great things to be found. Among his smaller piano pieces, there are commonplaces mingled with amazing ideas in the *Années de pélerinage,* but the *Hungarian Rhapsodies* are his least successful works.[308]

RAVEL was very perceptive:

> It is to Liszt's defects that Wagner owes his turgescence, Strauss his churlish enthusiasms, Franck his ponderous ideality, the Russians the tinsel which occasionally mars their picturesqueness. But it is also to him that all these dissimilar composers owe the best of their qualities.[309]

STRAVINSKY placed Liszt above Chopin and thought him a more interesting composer than Wagner. Liszt's immense talent as a composer, he said, is frequently underrated.[310]

Gustav Mahler
(1860–1911)

SCHOENBERG was an associate and admirer of Mahler. After a performance of Mahler's Fifth Symphony he wrote to the composer:

> I must not speak as a musician if I am to give any idea of the incredible impression your symphony made on me: I can speak only as one human being to another. For I saw your very soul, naked, stark naked. It was revealed to me as a stretch of wild and secret country, with eerie chasms and abysses neighboured by sunlit, smiling meadows, haunts of idyllic repose. I felt it as an event of nature, which after scourging us with its terrors puts a rainbow in the sky. What does it matter that what I was told afterwards of your "programme" did not seem to correspond altogether with what I had felt. Whether I am a good or bad indicator of the feelings an experience arouses in me is not the point. Must I have a correct understanding of what I have lived and felt? And I believe I felt your symphony. I shared in the battling for illusion; I suffered the pangs of disillusionment; I saw the forces of evil and good wrestling with each other; I saw a man in torment struggling towards inward harmony; I divined a personality, a drama, and *truthfulness,* the most uncompromising *truthfulness.*[311]

After Mahler's death Schoenberg wrote in memoriam:

> Gustav Mahler was a saint. Anyone who knew him even slightly must have had that feeling. Perhaps only a few understood it. And among even those few the only ones who have honored him were the men of goodwill. The others reacted to the saint as the wholly evil have always reacted to complete goodness and greatness: they martyred him. They carried things

so far that this great man doubted his own work. Not once was the cup allowed to pass away from him. He had to swallow even the most bitter one: the loss, if only temporarily, of his faith in his work.[312]

RICHARD STRAUSS wrote to Mahler after a rehearsal of the latter's Fifth Symphony that Strauss heard in Berlin in 1905:

> Your Fifth Symphony again gave me great pleasure in the full rehearsal, a pleasure only slightly dimmed by the little Adagietto. But as this was what pleased the audience most, you are getting what you deserve. The first two movements, especially, are quite magnificent; the Scherzo has a quality of genius but seemed rather too long.[313]

But Strauss and Mahler were never certain what to make of each other's music. In a letter to Hugo von Hofmannsthal, Strauss wrote: "I am open to all that is creative and have always, even amid the clamour of enthusiasts and sycophants, refused to countenance what is heterogeneous, hybrid and vague aspiration rather than solid achievement, as in Gustav Mahler's music, for instance."[314]

VAUGHAN WILLIAMS, in a passage in an autobiographical sketch, revealed his incompatibility with Mahler's music: "Intimate acquaintance with the executive side of music in orchestra, chorus and opera made even Mahler into a very tolerable imitation of a composer."[315]

KLEMPERER, great conductor and composer (of a kind), came under Mahler's influence as a young man and was a major interpreter of his music. He said: "I don't like everything he wrote. But most of it. I conducted the Fourth Symphony, the Seventh, the Ninth Symphony, *Das Lied von der Erde*. The First I conducted only once in my life, at Cologne, but I don't like at all the last movement. The Ninth Symphony I think the greatest."[316]

BOULEZ also conducts some of Mahler's compositions. He has written:

> What is it that attracts us about Mahler? Is it more the sentimental, bizarre or sarcastic reflexes of a dwindling world at the turn of the century which a keenly perspicacious man knew how to catch? Is this sufficient to hold our attention and enthral us? The reason for the fascination today surely lies in that hypnotic ability to project a vision that passionately embraces the end of an era; an era which inexorably had to wilt away so that another could be born in its place. This music describes the myth of the Phoenix almost too literally.[317]

COPLAND took another view:

> Mahler . . . admittedly, is long-winded, trite, bombastic, lacks taste and sometimes plagiarizes unblushingly, filching his material from Schubert,

Mozart, Bruckner. . . . But when all is said, there remains something extraordinarily touching about the man's work. . . . All his nine symphonies are suffused with personality. . . . The irascible Scherzos, the heaven-storming calls on the brass, the special quality of communing with nature . . . the gargantuan *Ländler,* the pages of incredible loneliness—all these, combined with histrionics, an inner warmth, and a will to evoke the largest forms and the grandest musical thoughts, add up to one of the most fascinating composer-personalities of modern times. . . . Mahler would be an important figure even if his music was not so engrossing [and] years in advance of its time.[318]

BERNSTEIN, who himself is one of the finest interpreters of Mahler's music today, has made this observation:

I suppose the easiest composer to interpret from a conductor's point of view is Mahler. And I mean easy in the sense that you can never be in doubt about what he wanted. . . . His is the most annotated music that anyone has ever tried to write. . . . You cannot possibly misunderstand Mahler's intentions.[319]

Bernstein also pointed out that despite the carping about how Mahler's music is derived from Mozart, Schubert, Wagner, and whomever, there can be no doubt that it always comes out sounding like Mahler, and that nobody else could have written it.[320]

All of Mahler's music is about Mahler—which means simply that it is about conflict. Think of it: Mahler the creator v. Mahler the performer; the Jew v. the Christian; the Believer v. the Doubter; the Naïf v. the Sophisticate; the provincial Bohemian v. the Viennese *homme du monde;* the Faustian Philosopher v. the Oriental Mystic; the operatic symphonist who never wrote an opera. But mainly the battle rages between Western Man at the turn of the century and the life of the spirit. Out of this opposition proceeds the endless list of antitheses—the whole roster of Yang and Ying—that inhabits Mahler's music.[321]

Finally, SCHOENBERG once said: "If you are in a position to observe the way Mahler ties his tie, you can learn more counterpoint from this than you can in three years at the conservatory."[322]

Pietro Mascagni
(1863–1945)

VERDI characteristically recognized the virtues and faults of Mascagni the musician:

> Mascagni possesses a very great talent, he composes and invents with admirable ease, spontaneity and *élan*; but I believe that we, the old school, from Rossini on, studied music more, acquired a more thorough knowledge of harmony and therefore had at our disposal a greater variety of expression for different situations, without which one runs the risk of employing identical effects for different emotions.[323]

Jules Massenet
(1842–1912)

DEBUSSY was very scathing about Massenet's opera, *Werther*, writing that everything in it was second-hand, and that Massenet pandered "to stupid ideas and amateur standards." He declared that Massenet's treatment of the subject, fine and genuine in itself, transforms it into a "sentimental mockery of itself."[324]

Felix Mendelssohn-Bartholdy
(1809–1847)

BERLIOZ was an admirer of Mendelssohn, as these quotations from his letters show:

> His talent is enormous, extraordinary, superb, prodigious. You can't suspect me of partiality in saying this, for he frankly told me that he understood nothing of my music.[325]

> I have made the acquaintance of Mendelssohn. He is a wonderful fellow. His skill as a player is as great as his genius, which is saying a great deal. I am convinced that he is one of the greatest musical talents of the age.[326]

> I have heard poor Mendelssohn's last oratorio, *Elijah*. It is magnificently grand and indescribably sumptuous in harmony.[327]

SCHUMANN knew and had a great affection for Mendelssohn. In a letter to Clara Wieck he wrote that Mendelssohn was the most eminent man he had met so far in his life. He thought that he could learn from him for years, but, he added, Mendelssohn could also learn something from him.[328] Schumann also said that Mendelssohn was "the Mozart of the nineteenth century," a brilliant musician able to see clearly and reconcile the contradictions of the period.[329]

In 1848 LISZT passed through Dresden and there met Schumann and Wagner, among others, one evening. Liszt discussed the relative merits of Meyerbeer and Mendelssohn to the latter's disadvantage, which was too much for SCHUMANN. He shouted at Liszt: "Meyerbeer is a nonentity compared with Mendelssohn! Mendelssohn's influence has been felt over the whole world, and you would do better to hold your tongue!" With that Schumann stormed out of the room.[330]

WAGNER'S attitude to Mendelssohn's music was confused by his extraordinary view that it was not within the capacity of a Jew to write great music—his anti-Semitism, in fact. Wagner wrote:

> In hearing a tone-piece of this composer, we have only been able to feel engrossed where nothing beyond our more or less amusement-craving phantasy was roused through the presentation, stringing-together, and entanglement of the most elegant, the smoothest and most polished figures—as in the kaleidoscope's changeful play of form and colour—but never where those figures were meant to take the shape of deep and stalwart feelings of the human heart.[331]

Wagner also disapproved of Mendelssohn the conductor:

> Mendelssohn's performance of Beethoven's works was always based only upon their purely musical side, and never upon their poetical contents, which he could not grasp at all.[332]

SIBELIUS spoke of Mendelssohn:

> After Bach, Mendelssohn was the greatest master of fugue. It sounds strange, maybe, but nevertheless it's true.

> Even today, Mozart and Mendelssohn are unrivalled in respect of orchestration. . . . Mozart and Mendelssohn did not use the instruments of today. What would they not have achieved if they had lived now![333]

Olivier Messiaen
(b. 1908)

Messiaen was the teacher of BOULEZ at the Paris Conservatoire; Boulez said of him that "between the wars there was only one great French composer—Messiaen."[334] His initial awe of Messiaen did not last; later he said: "Messiaen never really interested me. His use of certain Indian and Greek rhythms poses a problem—at least to me. It is difficult to retrieve pieces of another civilisation in a work. We must invent our own rhythmic vocabulary, following the norms that are our own."[335]

STRAVINSKY was somewhat sarcastic about Messiaen's music:

> One of those great hymns of his might be the wisest choice of all our music for the deck-band concert on the *Titanic* of our sinking civilisation; among other advantages, rescuing vessels—other planets—would have a good chance of hearing it.[336]

Also:

> *Couleurs de la cité céleste* [of Messiaen] came my way recently. It seemed to have been inspired by J. Arthur Rank, and its *force de frappe* is so great I wonder the marimbas, xylophones, cymbals and gongs do not collapse from metal fatigue.[337]

But Stravinsky also said: "I unrashly predict, as well, that his more recent works will last as long as any music of the time."[338]

LUTOSŁAWSKI said very recently:

> Of the composers who can certainly be expected to stand the test of time I would mention first Olivier Messiaen. He creates much that is "new,"

but at the same time he is his own self in everything he does. He has his very own idiom, his own musical world within which he moves. And even though he is not expanding this world, nevertheless his music is of value as such, because all his works contain a certain message, one of lasting worth. He creates music with a future I can believe in.[339]

Claudio Monteverdi
(1567–1643)

The great Italian Monteverdi stood midway between the Renaissance and the Baroque eras, but his music was scarcely known in the twentieth century until the 1930s. COPLAND wrote in 1953: "The first of the great opera composers was the Italian Claudio Monteverdi. Unfortunately, his works are rarely given nowadays and would strike our present-day opera lovers as little more than museum pieces if they were performed."[340] Thirty-five years later, *Orfeo* and *L'incoronazione di Poppea* have almost become repertory operas. STRAVINSKY made this observation, apparently having heard much more of Monteverdi's music than had Copland: "He is probably the first musician to whom we *can* feel very close."[341]

Wolfgang Amadeus Mozart
(1756–1791)

HAYDN was a dear and close friend of Mozart. In a letter to his daughter, Wolfgang's sister, Leopold Mozart reported a remark that Haydn had said to him:

> Before God and as an honest man I tell you that your son is the greatest composer known to me either in person or by name. He has taste and, what is more, the most profound knowledge of composition.[342]

Haydn also wrote this in a letter to Roth in Prague:

> If I could only persuade every friend of music, but especially the great ones, to understand and to feel Mozart's inimitable works as deeply as I do and to study them with as great feeling and musical understanding as I give to them. If I could, how the cities would compete to possess such peerlessness within their walls. Prague would do well to keep a firm grip on this wonderful man—but also to reward him with treasures. For unless they are rewarded, the life of great geniuses is sorrowful and, alas, affords little encouragement to posterity to strive more nobly; for that reason so many promising spirits succumb.... It angers me that this unique man Mozart has not yet been engaged by some imperial or royal court.[343]

BEETHOVEN'S respect for Mozart was immense. Ferdinand Ries, a friend of Beethoven, observed that of all composers Beethoven valued most highly Mozart and Handel, then J. S. Bach: "Whenever I found him with music in his hand or lying on his desk it was surely compositions of these heroes. Haydn seldom escaped without a few sly thrusts."[344] Thayer records in his great biography several comments by Beethoven on works of Mozart. He loved especially the Piano Concerto in D Minor, K. 466, for which he wrote cadenzas. Once when he heard the Piano Concerto in C Minor, K. 491, he directed his companion Cramer to the simple but beautiful motive that is first introduced towards the end of the work and exclaimed: "Cramer, Cramer! We shall never be able to do anything like that!"[345]

Beethoven was asked once by the Baroness Born which of Mozart's operas he thought the most of. "*Die Zauberflöte*," said Beethoven, and suddenly clasping his hands and throwing up his eyes he exclaimed, "Oh, Mozart!"[346] On the other hand, he was critical of *Don Giovanni*, saying: "Our sacred art ought never to permit itself to be degraded to the position of being a foil for so scandalous a subject."[347] Yet in a letter Beethoven wrote: "The good reception of Mozart's *Don Juan* [i.e., *Don Giovanni*] gives as much pleasure as if it were my own work."[348] Thayer also reports Czerny, who was a pupil of Beethoven, as saying that Beethoven was sometimes inexhaustible in his praise of Mozart. In a letter to Abbé Stadler, Beethoven wrote: "Always have I reckoned myself among the greatest admirers of Mozart and I will remain until my last breath."[349]

SARTI, the Italian composer whom Mozart quoted in the supper scene in act 2 of *Don Giovanni*, wrote this of two string quartets of Mozart:

> From these two fragments [from the Quartets in D Minor, K.421, and C Major, K.465] we can decide that the composer (whom I do not know and do not want to know) is only a piano player with a depraved ear; he is a sectary of the false system that divides the octave into twelve equal semitones, a system sufficiently well known to intelligent artists, and one proved false by harmonic science.
>
> Could a sound taste allow the first violin to enter so dissonantly as in the second and sixth bars of the first quotation [i.e., in the introduction to the C Major Quartet]? Has the composer done it to cover the player with shame, or so that the hearers may cry out: "He is out of tune"? Is this the best way to write music? In short, if this composer packs his works with such capital errors (19 in 36 bars) as he has been shown to have done in these two fragments, we may be sure that they will be rejected by everyone who has a good and unspoilt ear.[350]

SCHUBERT wrote in his diary on 13 June 1816:

> All my life I shall remember this fine, clear, lovely day. I shall hear softly, as from a distance, the magic strains of Mozart's music. . . . In the dark places of this life they point to that clear-shining and distant future in which our whole hope lies. O Mozart, immortal Mozart, how many, how infinitely many inspiring suggestions of a finer, better life have you left in our souls![351]

BERLIOZ commented about Mozart in his memoirs:

> The marvellous beauty of his quartets and quintets and of one or two of
> the sonatas was what first converted me to this celestial genius, which
> thenceforth I worshipped while regretting that his admired association
> with Italians and learned contrapuntalists had even slightly tarnished its
> purity.[352]

ROSSINI is reported to have said that Beethoven is a colossus who often
gives you a dig in the ribs, but it is Mozart who is always adorable, because
he had the chance of visiting Italy at the time when the Italians sang well.[353]
Asked his opinion about the great Italian composers, Rossini replied that
the greatest was Mozart, although he was a foreigner. Mozart was very
skilled in composition, he said, made himself Italian in song, and could
deal admirably with both the serious and the facetious, something not given
to everybody.[354] Rossini is said by Stravinsky to have remarked: "Mozart
was the delight of my youth, the desperation of my maturity, and the
consolation of my old age."[355]

BRAHMS venerated Mozart, especially the operas, and possessed the
manuscript of the Symphony No. 40 in G Minor. In 1896, just prior to his
death, he went to Berlin to conduct his two piano concertos and attended
a dinner given by Joachim. The violinist proposed the toast to "the most
famous composer," but Brahms interposed hastily, "Quite right: here's to
Mozart!" and clinked glasses all round.[356]

Cosima Wagner recorded in her diary that WAGNER and she went
through the last scene of *Le nozze di Figaro* and afterward read the same
scene in Beaumarchais. They "once again felt the transfiguring influence
of the music. In the play they are like beetles, struggling laboriously on
the ground, in the opera they are butterflies playing in the air."[357]

TCHAIKOVSKY was another composer who adored Mozart. He wrote
in his diaries: "I love everything in Mozart, for we love everything in the
man to whom we are truly devoted. Above all, *Don Giovanni,* for through
that work I have learnt to know what music is."[358] BIZET remarked that
"Mozart's music affects me so directly that it actually makes me feel
sick."[359]

RAVEL revered Mozart above all other composers. He saw Mozart as
superhuman in the clarity, perfection of his workmanship, and the purity
of his lyricism, not to mention his prodigious output. He also saw in Mozart's work a striking balance between classical symmetry and the element
of surprise, of the unexpected, and this union of symmetry and surprise
was to remain a key aspect of Ravel's artistic aspirations.[360] Ravel wrote
in a letter:

> I have never felt the need to formulate, either for the benefit of others
> or for myself, the principles of my aesthetic. If I were ever called upon

to do so, I would ask to be allowed to identify myself with the simple pronouncements made by Mozart on the subject. He confined himself to saying that there is nothing that music can not undertake to do, or dare, or portray, provided it continues to charm and always remains music.[361]

The French pianist Gaby Casadesus recalled that Ravel liked the Bee-
.thoven string quartets, but said: "If you look at the Mozart quartets they are much more interesting than the Beethoven. And the concertos. . . . You have only five concertos by Beethoven, but look at how many you have by Mozart."[362]

SCHNABEL, the great pianist and interpreter of Mozart, who was also a composer, wrote:

> Children have at least one very important element in common with Mo-
> zart, namely purity. They are not yet spoiled and prejudiced and person-
> ally involved. But these are, of course, not the reasons why their teachers
> give them Mozart to play. Children are given Mozart because of the small
> quantity of the notes; the grown-ups avoid Mozart because of the great
> quality of the notes—which, to be true, is elusive.[363]

SIBELIUS regarded Mozart as the greatest master of orchestration and several times mentioned that the G Minor Symphony had run through his life like a thread. He said: "The Finale is especially marvellous. I would like to hear that at the time of my death." Sibelius also is recorded as saying: "When Mozart takes his farewell of a theme there is always something that is melancholy—particularly in the *Adagios*."[364]

BERNSTEIN has also commented on the Symphony No. 40 in G Minor: "No amount of analysis or explanation can prepare one for the overwhelming surprise of its existence when it is actually heard in performance. It is hard to think of another work that so perfectly marries form and passion."[365]

COPLAND gave another present-day composer's reaction to Mozart's music:

> Paul Valéry once wrote: "The definition of beauty is easy: it is that which
> makes us despair." On reading that phrase, I immediately thought of
> Mozart. Admittedly, despair is an unusual word to couple with the Vi-
> ennese master's music. And yet, isn't it true that any incommensurate
> thing sets up within us a kind of despair? There is no way to *seize* the
> Mozart music. This is true even for a fellow-composer, any composer—
> who, being a composer, with a special sense of kinship, has even a happy
> familiarity, with the hero of Salzburg. After all, we can pore over him,
> dissect him, marvel or carp at him. But in the end there remains something
> that will not be *seized*. That is why, each time a Mozart work begins—I
> am thinking of the finest examples now—we composers listen with a
> certain awe and wonder, not unmixed with despair. The wonder we share

with everyone; the despair comes from the realisation that only this one man at this one moment in musical history could have created works that seem so effortless and so close to perfection.[366]

BRITTEN conducted *Idomeneo* at the Aldeburgh Festival in 1970 and at that time commented:

> My approach to Mozart derives essentially from my tremendous sympathy with and passion for his music. . . . In *Idomeneo*, and all his mature operas, there is nothing that is merely illustrative; everything derives from situation and character. Then there's that essential in all music, the phrasing. But, I think, most important of all is a passionate involvement and a realisation, with *Idomeneo*, of how a man of 25 could understand so marvellously the father-son relationship or how he could have created a character so close to Euripides as Elektra.[367]

MESSIAEN regards Mozart as the greatest rhythmician in classical music. With Mozart rhythm had a kinematic aspect derived from word and speech. The use of rhythmic groups in Mozart's work is so important that if the exact placement of the accents is not observed, the music is completely destroyed. For this reason there are so many bad interpretations of Mozart, as most musicians are not well enough educated in rhythm to discern the position of the accents.[368] Messiaen is convinced that Mozart's use of rhythm was quite conscious, as it is too consistent in his music not to have been premeditated.[369]

The odd man out among composers was DELIUS, who said: "If a man tells me he likes Mozart I know in advance he's a bad musician."[370] So as not to leave Mozart on this note, we will add SHOSTAKOVICH, who said that GLAZUNOV had told him that the Finale of the *Jupiter* Symphony was like Cologne Cathedral. "Honestly," said Shostakovich, "to this day I can't think of a better description of that amazing music."[371] And finally *ROSSINI*: "I take Beethoven twice a week, Haydn four times, and Mozart every day."[372]

Modest Mussorgsky
(1839–1881)

In an autobiographical note MUSSORGSKY said this of himself:

> Mussorgsky cannot be classed with any existing group of musicians, either by the character of his compositions or by his musical views. The formula of his artistic *profession de foi* may be explained by his view, as a composer, of the task of art: art as a means of communicating with the people, not an aim in itself.[373]

A problem that has bedevilled musicologists and performers has been the perceived need by Rimsky-Korsakov, Glazunov, Shostakovich, and others to edit, to complete, and on occasion to rewrite Mussorgsky's music. After Mussorgsky's death RIMSKY-KORSAKOV wrote:

> If Mussorgsky's compositions are fated to last unfaded for fifty years after his death, then an archaeologically exact edition can be used. In the meantime what was needed was an edition for performance, for practical artistic purposes, for the making known of his great talent, not for the study of his personality and artistic transgressions.[374]

CUI, one of the "Mighty Five," as was Mussorgsky, thought little of *Boris Godunov:* "There are these chief defects in *Boris Godunov:* chopped recitative and looseness of musical discourse, resulting in the effect of a potpourri. . . . These defects are the consequence of immaturity, indiscriminating, self-complacent, hasty method of composition."[375]

SHOSTAKOVICH said that he and Mussorgsky had a "special relationship"; "I revere Mussorgsky," he said, "I consider him one of the greatest Russian composers."[376] But this did not prevent Shostakovich from producing his own performing edition of *Boris Godunov*. STRAVINSKY saw no need to edit Mussorgsky's original score: "I think that in spite of his limited technical means and 'awkward writing,' his original scores always show infinitely more true musical interest and genuine intuition than the 'perfection' of Rimsky's 'learned' arrangements."[377]

TCHAIKOVSKY had a very poor opinion of Mussorgsky's operas. He wrote this of *Boris Godunov:* "I have made a thorough study of *Boris Godunov.* . . . I consign it from the bottom of my heart to the devil; it is the most insipid and base parody on music,"[378] and of *Khovanshchina,* "I discovered what I expected: pretensions to realism, original conceptions and methods, wretched technique, poverty of invention, occasionally clever episodes, amid an ocean of harmonic absurdities and affectations."[379] Tchaikovsky also wrote about Mussorgsky:

> His nature is narrow-minded, devoid of any urge towards self-perfection, blindly believing in the ridiculous theories of his circle and in his own genius. He has a certain base side to his nature which likes coarseness, uncouthness, roughness. He flaunts his illiteracy, takes pride in his ignorance, mucks along anyhow, blindly believing in the infallibility of his genius. Yet he has flashes of talent which are, moreover, not devoid of originality.[380]

However, DEBUSSY said that "Mussorgsky is unique and will remain so, for his art is free from artifice and arid formulae."[381] He also wrote:

> Never has a more refined sensibility expressed itself by simpler means: it seems to be the doing of some curious savage led by nothing but his emotion to discover step by step what music is about. "Form" is for him of no use whatever—or rather, the form he resorts to is everchanging to the point of being quite unlike any of the established, so to speak administrative, forms. His music, drawn by light touches, holds together by some mysterious link between them—and by his gift of luminous clearsightedness. Sometimes again Mussorgsky hints at quivering shades that unfold and wring the heart.[382]

Carl Nielsen
(1865–1931)

BERNSTEIN recorded Nielsen's Third Symphony (the *Sinfonia espansiva*) with the Royal Danish Orchestra in Copenhagen in 1965. At that time he wrote:

> Nielsen's music was never quite nationalistic enough to have become the definitive Danish music. Nor was [his] music international enough to take its place next to the Beethovens of the world. It . . . is an odd mixture of past and future, of tradition and prophecy. . . . But what makes it always sound like Nielsen is its total unpredictability. . . . I think many people are in for a pleasant surprise as they get to know Nielsen: his rough charm, his swing, his drive, his rhythmic surprises, his strange power of harmonic and tonal relationships, all of these are irresistible. I feel confident that Nielsen's time has come.[383]

Jacques Offenbach
(1819–1880)

At a performance of Offenbach's *Les Contes d'Hoffmann* at the Ring-
theater in Vienna in 1881, a fire broke out and 900 people lost their lives.
WAGNER was reported to have said after the catastrophe:

> All the people sitting together in such a theatre are mere good-for-noth-
> ings. When miners in a coal pit are buried alive, I am deeply moved and
> horrified, and I am filled with disgust for a society which obtains its means
> of heating in such a manner. But it leaves me cold, and hardly moves me,
> when a certain number of that crowd perish while listening to an Offenbach
> operetta which does not offer one iota of moral worth.[384]

MAHLER, on the other hand, had another view of the opera:

> It's a work of which I'm very fond. All through his life Offenbach strove
> to escape from operetta and to create opera. He succeeded in doing so
> only in his old age, when he was at death's door. Such is the fate of every
> one of us: we don't fulfill our dreams until we are about to die.[385]

Giovanni Palestrina
(c. 1525–1594)

VERDI was an ardent admirer of Palestrina and regarded him as the "cornerstone of Italian music."[386] He said that "music as we understand it begins with Palestrina: prior to that we neither know nor can we know what it is."[387] In his letters he wrote that Palestrina "is the real king of sacred music, and the Eternal Father of Italian music,"[388] and "I join you in praise of the three giants: Palestrina, Bach and Beethoven. When I think of the petty, poverty-stricken melody and harmony of our times, Palestrina seems a miracle."[389]

GOUNOD wrote after he had heard a mass of Palestrina's at St. Peter's in Rome of "that persistent and wonderful network of voices, those harmonic vibrations in the upper registers, that almost visionary sound of the greatest Christian temple in existence, all of which carries the soul beyond reality and uplifts it in exaltation."[390] After hearing a mass by Palestrina, DEBUSSY called it a marvel. The music, he said, was extremely pure and its feeling was conveyed by melodic arabesques, which combined with the shape and the outline to produce unique melodic harmonies.[391]

SATIE, too, was impressed, this time by a motet of Palestrina's:

> The religious feeling in this passage is immense. Yet the musical inspiration of each part is very simple. I feel that the ecstatic charm shown here results from the vocal inter-crossings. In any case I can see here one of the characteristics of Palestrina's transparent style. The angelic musician must have been one of the greatest believers who ever existed. He is always close to God; his manner is holy; his genius is benevolent. Here

truly is the charming son of our sweet religion, of that wonderful and imperishable Catholicism. Here is the brother of our dear cathedrals, of our Roman Christian Art, of all we love, of all we worship.[392]

Sergey Prokofiev
(1891–1953)

SHOSTAKOVICH was ambivalent towards his fellow Soviet composer Prokofiev. In reminiscences about him Shostakovich wrote that he had a deep insight into the life around him and had the means of expression to convey the full range of human emotions. He wrote with inimitable mastery scenes of human suffering that reach supreme heights, such as the death of Andrei Bolkonsky in the opera *War and Peace* and the finale of the second act and the death of Juliet in the ballet *Romeo and Juliet*. The love scenes in *War and Peace* throb with warmth and feeling, as do the scene of the Prince and Cinderella in the ballet *Cinderella*, the scene in Friar Lawrence's cell and the farewell scene in *Romeo and Juliet*, and the lullaby in the oratorio *On Guard for Peace*. In the heroic scenes in *War and Peace* and in the finale of the cantata *Alexander Nevsky* there is majesty and grandeur, and there is also sparkling humor in the opera *The Duenna*, in *Lieutenant Kije,* and in some of the ballets.[393] On the other hand, towards the end of his life Shostakovich said:

> I'm rather indifferent to Prokofiev's music now and listen to his compositions without any particular pleasure. I suppose *The Gambler* is the opera of his that I like the most, but even it has too many superficial random effects. Prokofiev sacrificed essential things too often for a flashy effect.[394]

STRAVINSKY'S view of Prokofiev was this:

> Prokofiev was the contrary of a musical thinker. He was, in fact, startlingly naive in matters of musical construction. He had some technique and

could do certain things very well, but more than that, he had personality; one saw it in his very gestures, biological personality let us call it. His musical judgements were usually commonplace, however, and often wrong. . . . But one could see Prokofiev a thousand times without establishing any profound connection with him, and we rarely discussed music when we were together. I used to think that Prokofiev's depths were engaged only when he played chess.[395]

COPLAND compared Prokofiev with Stravinsky: "Serge Prokofiev works a seemingly inexhaustible melodic mine as compared with Stravinsky's, yet few would claim him to be the more profound musical creator."[396]

Another Soviet contemporary of Prokofiev, KHACHATURIAN, wrote after the former's death:

What is the secret of the great charm of Prokofiev's melodies? His themes are an amazingly natural combination of the austere, masculine diatonic with rich chromaticism and bold, startling shifts in modulation. At the same time, his melodies are markedly Russian in flavour, broad flowing song motifs. The bold, sharply-etched themes of the epic *Alexander Nevsky*, the hearty *Toast to Stalin*, *Romeo and Juliet*, the enchanting cradle song from the *On Guard for Peace* oratorio, the vigorous sculptured motif of the Mistress of the Copper Mountain, the richly melodious Seventh Symphony—are among the melodies that come to my mind. The list could be greatly extended, yet these works alone place Prokofiev alongside the greatest masters of melody.[397]

The Italian MALIPIERO wrote:

It is impossible to classify the personality of Sergey Prokofiev, for he is neither the leader of a school, nor an innovator. It must surely be a difficult job for any critic to attempt to analyse him, or place him in any way in a period or a movement.[398]

Writing in 1927, SCHMITT said:

The *Classical Symphony* is an enchantment; a sort of unpublished Mozart, it possesses all his grace, fluidity, and divine perfection; and the orchestration streams out in crystal jets. It would be impossible to achieve a pastiche with more ingenuity or science. For in the case of Monsieur Prokofiev, the complete artist, knowledge equals imagination.[399]

After the première of Prokofiev's Fourth Symphony, SAUGUET wrote:

The Symphony No. 4 provides important evidence of what I believe to be the truth. This work is remarkable for its modesty. I mean that the composer has allowed the very lovely music to express itself quite natu-

rally, without constraint, without any external strivings after color, pic-
turesque motifs, scholarly developments—in fact without any regard for
any kind of modernism or aestheticism.[400]

Giacomo Puccini
(1858–1924)

The immensely popular opera composer Puccini attracted both the highest praise and the loudest condemnation from his fellow composers. The conductor Manuel Rosenthal said in an interview:

> One day Ravel was speaking to me in glowing terms about Puccini. And being the silly impertinent young man I was, I started to sneer. At that Ravel flew into a towering rage, locked us both into his little studio at Montfort l'Amaury and sat down at the piano. He then played the whole of *Tosca* from memory, stopping about fifty times on the way to ask, "Have you anything to complain about that passage? Look how good the harmony is, how he respects the form, what a clever, original and interesting modulation there is in that tune!" Finally he took down the score to show me how perfect the orchestration is. He said, "This is exactly what I did with *Le Tombeau de Couperin:* this economy of means by which two solo instruments in Puccini's orchestra produce such an impact—that is the mark of a great artist!"[401]

MAHLER was no admirer of Puccini. During a performance of *La Bohème* in Vienna he laughed derisively throughout. Then, about *Tosca,* he wrote to his wife Alma:

> Last night there was my visit to the opera: *Tosca,* as I told you. An excellent production in every way; quite an eye-opener, for a provincial town in Austria. But as for the work itself! Act I, papal pageantry with continual chiming of bells (especially imported from Italy). Act 2, A man tortured; horrible cries. Another stabbed with a bread knife. Act 3. More of the magnificent tintabulations [*sic*] and a view over all Rome from the

citadel. Followed by an entirely fresh onset of bell ringing. A man shot by a firing party. I got up before the shooting and went out. Needless to say, a masterpiece. Nowadays any bungler orchestrates to perfection.[402]

Although Puccini was the successor to VERDI in the field of Italian opera, there is only one reference to him in all of Verdi's correspondence. This is in a letter to Conte Opprandino Arrivabene:

I have heard the composer Puccini highly spoken of. He follows the modern trends, which is natural, but he keeps to melody which is neither ancient or modern. However the symphonic vein appears to predominate in him. No harm in that, but one needs to tread carefully here. Opera is opera and symphony symphony and I don't think it is a good thing to put a symphonic piece into an opera merely to put the orchestra through its paces.[403]

STRAVINSKY was scathing about *La fanciulla del West,* remarking on "the unsuitability of the subject to that genius of sentimentality which in *La Bohème* is so perfectly matched to the dramatic substance."[404]

BRITTEN too could not be counted among Puccini's admirers. "What do you think of Puccini?" SHOSTAKOVICH once asked him. "His operas are dreadful." "No, Ben, you're wrong," said Shostakovich. "He wrote marvellous operas but dreadful music." Writing about *La Bohème,* Britten said: "I was not surprised that after four or five performances I never wanted to hear *La Bohème* again. In spite of its neatness, I became sickened by the cheapness and emptiness of the music."[405]

Sergey Rachmaninov
(1873–1943)

Rachmaninov's First Symphony was premiered in Moscow in 1897, but it was condemned by critics and was never performed again in the composer's lifetime. He wrote nothing of importance for the next two years. One who wrote about the symphony was CUI:

> If there were a conservatory in Hell, if one of its talented students were instructed to write a programme symphony on the "Seven Plagues of Egypt", and if he were to compose a symphony like Mr. Rachmaninov's, then he would have fulfilled his task brilliantly and would bring delight to the inhabitants of Hell.[406]

MEDTNER, the Russian composer and pianist, who was a colleague of Rachmaninov's—his music has been described as "poor man's Rachmaninov"—wrote about him in 1933:

> It is precisely because of his fame that it is difficult to speak of Rachmaninov. This fame is more than his: it is the glory of our art. This rare identification of his personal fame with our whole art is evidence of the authenticity of our inspiration. This unbroken contact of his entire being with art itself can be sensed each time his touch produces sound. This sound, in score or keyboard, is never neutral, impersonal, empty. It is as distinct from other sounds as a bell is different from street noises; it is the result of incomparable intensity, flame, and the saturation of beauty.[407]

Maurice Ravel
(1875–1937)

After he heard of Ravel's death, PROKOFIEV wrote:

> The world has lost one of the greatest composers of the age. Not all musicians, I am sure, fully appreciate as yet the magnitude of his talent. While continuing to some extent the creative style of Debussy, Ravel contributed to music much that was highly individual and original. . . . There was a time shortly after the war when a group of young musicians in France—Honegger, Milhaud, Poulenc and several others—declared that Ravel's music had outlived its time, that new composers and a new musical idiom had appeared on the scene. The years passed, the new composers have taken their allotted places in French music, but Ravel still remains one of the leading French composers and one of the outstanding musicians of our time.[408]

The Italian CASELLA also wrote at that time of Ravel:

> Even the most uncompromising foes were ultimately compelled to acknowledge his technical mastery and his sense of form. His music, for technical perfection, ranks with Bach's, Mozart's and Chopin's. His mentality was fundamentally scholastic—an idiosyncrasy betrayed by his fondness for contrapuntal artifices such as fugue, stretti, inversions, canons, and so on. His inclination to start from some musical model—to place himself in front of a Mozart sonata or a Saint-Saëns concerto as a painter in front of a landscape or sitter—has often been mentioned. The wonder is that the outcome was always thoroughly original and unlike the model.

> He composed for the élite around him, never believing that there could be two kinds of music—one for the upper classes and another for the

proletarians. The last time I saw him, three years ago, as I was alluding to the popularity of his works, he said to me: "Well, we must not exaggerate: but if instead of nourishing the masses on old commonplaces one attempted to foster in them a sense for true music, they would respond." I never heard him judge a brother composer unfairly. Contrary to most composers, he was a keen admirer of talent wherever he found it; and his mind was as free from jealously as it was cultured and alert.[409]

Much earlier, in 1919, KODÁLY wrote:

> This interesting composer belongs to the new French school, but though Debussy is its starting point, and though he shares many of his peculiarities of style, he is not to be regarded simply as an imitator. In Ravel, the incorporeal, ethereal music of Debussy is infused with an alien element, a savage determination which, though maybe it brings him closer to the world of everyday experience, prevents him from achieving so often the poetic quality of his master.[410]

Despite his remarks quoted earlier, PROKOFIEV was critical of Ravel's ballet suite *Daphnis et Chloé*: "Incredibly boring, thin and watery, soporific when it touches on poetry, and laughable when it concerns drama or scenic action. Its success is due entirely to its enchanting choreography."[411] Later Prokofiev remarked that *Boléro* was a miracle in mastery of composition and spoke of the charm of Ravel's String Quartet, as well as his extraordinary art in using national French and Spanish songs. He said: "If some of Ravel's compositions are marked by extreme fineness of style, which we oppose here [in Soviet Russia] with more virile, buoyant, and joyous emotions, still, we can and should learn a great deal from his works both in virtuoso orchestration and harmony."[412]

STRAVINSKY paid tribute to Ravel, saying that his "musical judgment was very acute" and "I would say that he was the only musician who immediately understood *Le Sacre du printemps.*"[413] About *Daphnis et Chloé* Stravinsky said that "not only is it one of Ravel's greatest achievements, it is one of the finest things in French music."[414]

FALLA, the Spanish composer, pointed out: "When [Ravel] wanted to characterize Spain musically, he showed a predilection for the *habanera,* the song most in vogue when his mother lived in Madrid. . . . That is why the rhythm, much to the surprise of the Spaniards, went on living in French music although Spain had forgotten it half a century ago."[415]

Ravel admired GERSHWIN'S *Rhapsody in Blue.* When the two composers met in France, Gershwin, who greatly admired Ravel, asked if he could study with him. Ravel refused, saying: "You would only lose the spontaneous quality of your melody and end by writing bad Ravel."[416]

LAMBERT said of *Boléro:* "There is a definite limit to the length of time a composer can go on writing in one dance rhythm. This limit is obviously reached by Ravel toward the end of *La Valse* and toward the beginning of *Boléro*."[417] Ravel himself said to Honegger: "I've written only one masterpiece—*Boléro*. Unfortunately there's no music in it."[418] When Ravel was told that at the première of *Boléro* a lady had called out: "He is mad!" he answered, smiling, that she understood the piece.[419]

VAUGHAN WILLIAMS studied with Ravel in Paris in 1908. Ravel told him that the heavy contrapuntal Teutonic manner was not necessary; his motto was "Complexe, mais pas compliqué." According to Vaughan Williams, Ravel was opposed to development for its own sake and believed that "one should only develop for the sake of arriving at something better."[420]

Nikolay Rimsky-Korsakov
(1844–1908)

RACHMANINOV, who was a conductor as well as composer and pianist, much admired Rimsky-Korsakov's skill as an orchestrator. He said on different occasions:

> When I was conductor at the Bolshoi Theatre I put on Rimsky's *Pan Voyevoda*. The music is poor but the orchestration—stupendous.[421]

> His mastery of the technique of composition, especially his skill in instrumentation and his sensitive control of true color, filled me with admiration.[422]

> What untold riches there are in *Coq d'Or!* The beginning alone—how novel. And then the chromaticism. This is where the source of all the wretched modernism is hidden. But with Rimsky it is in the hands of a genius.[423]

Rimsky-Korsakov was STRAVINSKY'S teacher at St. Petersburg. Later in his life Stravinsky said: "My master, Rimsky-Korsakov, was tall and severe, a man with eye-glasses and a redingote. He had a profound respect for the classical rules of musical composition, and he did not always approve of what I was doing."[424] In 1944 Stravinsky prepared a statement for Rimsky-Korsakov's centenary to be broadcast in Russia: "Not only in a tribute to his genius but gratefully for his loving, unforgettable, fatherly guidance in the very inception of my creative musical life: To the master and man whom I love, I bow."[425] Stravinsky, in his autobiography, pointed out the rigor and frankness of Rimsky-Korsakov's judgment when his verdict as to the musical vocation of a beginner was required: "The story was told of a young doctor who came to show him his compositions and ask for advice. Having learned that he was a doctor, Rimsky-Korsakov said: 'Excellent. Continue to practise medicine.' "[426]

Gioacchino Rossini
(1792–1868)

Rossini visited BEETHOVEN in Vienna in 1822. Later, in 1860, Rossini told Wagner that Beethoven said to him: "So you are the composer of *Barbier von Seville?* It is an accomplished opera buffa. . . . Serious opera is not the business of Italians. . . . They are lacking in music theory. . . . but no one surpasses the Italians in opera buffa."[427] According to Karl Gottfried Freudenberg, Beethoven described Rossini as a "talented and melodious composer; his music suits the frivolous and sensuous spirit of the time, and his productivity is such that he needs only as many weeks as the Germans do years to write an opera."[428]

BERLIOZ wrote in his memoirs:

> Rossini's melodic cynicism, his contempt for dramatic expression and good sense, his endless repetition of a single form of cadence, his eternal puerile crescendo and brutal bass drum, exasperated me to such a point that I was blind to the brilliant qualities of his genius even in his masterpiece, *The Barber*, exquisitely scored though it is.[429]

DONIZETTI never regarded himself as Rossini's equal and wrote:

> Rossini is a genius and as such he has opened the imagination of his contemporaries. After him—I am speaking of Italy—every other composer lived or lives with the science and with the taste and with the practice born from the style created by his genius. Rossini appeared and accomplished that which was granted only to a genius to achieve. Although young and almost ignorant of Art, he divined the effects of Mozart in *Don Giovanni*, of Beethoven in the symphonies. . . . The public, shaken from a species of musical apathy, encouraged the new composer, and he,

much emboldened by his successes, endeavoured, and succeeded. . . . Not by study, but by frequent opportunity to write, he improved and made himself severely correct in his art. By means of so much genius, so much practice, and, in spite of himself, so much musical science, sprang *Guillaume Tell.*[430]

VERDI wrote after hearing *Guillaume Tell:* "Ah, Rossini! He was a man, and *he was himself!* He possessed a quality that is now lost, that none of us now have: he knew how to write for the voice. Look at the trio from *Guillaume Tell!*[431]

MENDELSSOHN visited Rossini in Frankfurt in 1836 and then wrote in a letter to his mother and sister:

Rossini, big, fat, and in the sunniest disposition of mind. I really know few men who can be so amusing and witty as he, when he chooses; he kept us laughing the whole time. I promised that the Cecilia Association would sing the B Minor Mass for him and several other works of Sebastian Bach. It will be quite too much fun to see Rossini obliged to admire Sebastian Bach. He thinks, however, "different countries, different customs", and is resolved to howl with the wolves. . . . Intellect, animation and wit sparkle in all his features and in every word, and whoever does not consider him a genius ought to hear him expiating in this way, in order to change his opinion.[432]

WAGNER commented: "Like Mozart, he possessed melodic inventiveness to the highest degree. Further, that inventiveness was marvellously seconded by his instinct for the stage and for dramatic expression. What might he not have produced if he had received a forceful and complete musical education?"[433]

BIZET wrote in a letter: "When I hear *Le nozze di Figaro* or the second act of *Guillaume Tell,* I am completely happy. I experience a sense of perfect well-being and satisfaction, I forget everything. Oh, how lucky one is to be thus favoured!"[434]

SHOSTAKOVICH'S Fifteenth Symphony has a direct quotation from the *Guillaume Tell* Overture; Shostakovich stated that that piece had been his earliest musical recollection.[435]

Let Rossini himself have the last word: "My immortality? Do you know what will survive me? The third act of *Tell,* the second act of *Otello,* and *The Barber of Seville* from one end to the other."[436]

Camille Saint-Saëns
(1835–1921)

Fellow Frenchman GOUNOD said of Saint-Saëns: "Monsieur Saint-Saëns possesses one of the most astonishing musical organisations I know of. He is a musician armed with every weapon. He is a master of his craft as no one else is. . . . He plays, and plays with the orchestra as he does the piano. One can say no more."[437]

HONEGGER saw the influence of Saint-Saëns on a later generation of French composers: "The surprise effect of a new discovery is quickly dispelled and one soon discovers behind the greatest innovators the masters who inspired them. Wagner stands behind Schoenberg, Rimsky behind Stravinsky, and behind Ravel there is Saint-Saëns."[438]

RAVEL admired Saint-Saëns's clarity, considering his piano concertos as perfect specimens of light music. But during World War I when Ravel himself was serving as a driver in the French army for a short while, he wrote: "I'm told that Saint-Saëns has informed a delighted public that since the war began he composed music for stage, melodies, an elegy and a piece for trombone. If he'd been making shell-cases instead it might have been all the better for music."[439]

D'INDY wrote that Saint-Saëns's Third Symphony, although displaying undoubted talent, appeared to challenge the traditional laws of tonal structure, and that despite the cleverness and eloquence of the composer and indisputed interest of the work, its final impression is that of doubt and sadness.[440]

Saint-Saëns was asked by Sir Thomas Beecham in 1913, after Beecham had led a performance of the Third Symphony in the composer's presence, what he thought of the interpretation. Saint-Saëns replied: "My dear young friend, I have lived a long while, and I have known all the chefs d'orchestre. There are two kinds: one takes the music too fast, and the other too slow. There is no third!"[441]

Erik Satie
(1866–1925)

STRAVINSKY described Satie: "He was a quick-witted fellow, shrewd, clever and mordant. Of his compositions I prefer above all his *Socrate* and certain pages of *Parade*."[442] Milhaud said that RAVEL did not like *Socrate* at all, and that he did not understand it. Ravel told Milhaud that he could never agree with a work which for him was so poor—in invention, poor in everything. "This sort of very pure line and very simple harmonies is far removed from the Ravelian aesthetic."[443]

DEBUSSY was a close friend of Satie, who had some influence on him. For his part, Satie once wrote: "If I didn't have Debussy . . . I don't know what I'd do to express my wretched thoughts—if I am still able to express them."[444] LAMBERT wrote: "If Satie's music is difficult to appreciate it is not due to any obscurity in his technical style, which is always clear-cut and limpid, but his habit of abruptly changing his mood within the course of a single bar."[445]

Domenico Scarlatti (1685–1757)

Scarlatti is best known for his hundreds of harpsichord sonatas. His important position in music was recognized by MALIPIERO, who was the editor of Monteverdi, Vivaldi, and other Italian composers. He wrote:

> Domenico Scarlatti is a precursor in the fullest sense of the word; all his means of expression spring from the virgin soil; they emanate solely from his mind. All the mannerisms, all the cadenza, all that became a habit in the music of the Italian 18th century and ended so powerfully individualizing it, appear for the first time in Domenico Scarlatti, and are his absolute invention.[446]

Arnold Schoenberg
(1874–1951)

The originator of atonality and a crucial figure in the history of music in the twentieth century, Schoenberg had his supporters and his detractors, apart from those who respected him but did not comprehend his method. MAHLER was one of the last, saying: "I don't understand his music, but he's young and perhaps he's right. I am old and I daresay my ear is not sensitive enough."[447] Mahler said about Schoenberg's First String Quartet: "I have conducted the most difficult scores of Wagner; I have written complicated music myself in scores of up to thirty staves and more; yet here is a score of not more than four staves, and I am unable to read them."[448]

RAVEL, who was born within a year of Schoenberg, wrote in an article about contemporary music:

> We have often heard or read that atonality is a blind alley leading nowhere, but I do not accept the validity of this opinion; because, while as a system it may be so, it certainly cannot as an influence. In fact, the influence of Schoenberg may be overwhelming on his followers, but the significance of his art is to be identified with influences of a more subtle kind—not the system, but the aesthetic, of his art. I am quite conscious of the fact that my *Chansons madécasses* are in no way Schoenbergian, but I do not know whether I ever should have been able to write them had Schoenberg never written.[449]

SIBELIUS, another contemporary, said: "I was one of the first to get hold of Arnold Schoenberg's works for myself. I bought them on Busoni's advice, to learn something. But I learned nothing."[450] Sibelius also said: "Alban Berg is Schoenberg's best achievement."[451]

DELIUS also could not accept the twelve-tone system: "You can't make music out of theories. When a man has to write about his methods of composition you may be sure he has nothing to say."[452] Also: "In my opinion there is no music without emotion; it is the first and last essential of beautiful music, and intellectuality must only play a secondary role. Ugly sounds are not music, nor have they anything to do with music."[453] And again:

> I have not heard *Pierrot Lunaire* but what I have heard of Schoenberg was either weak Brahms or weak Wagner, or very academically constructed ugly sounds. A monstrous orchestra does not make the *Gurrelieder* either strong or original. Musical theorists have as yet never been able to write beautiful music—whether they be called Busoni or Schoenberg. The real musical genius writes for no other purpose but to express his own soul, and in doing so finds life's greatest satisfaction and joy.[454]

STRAVINSKY, one of the other musical influences of the twentieth century, spoke or wrote about Schoenberg often. These remarks he made in 1936:

> Schoenberg, in my judgment, is more of a chemist of music than an artistic creator. His investigations are important, since they tend to expand the possibilities of auditory enjoyment, but . . . they are more concerned with the quantitative rather than the qualitative aspects of music. The value of this is evident but limited, since others will come later and look for and find "eighth-tones", but will they be able to make genuine works of art out of this? I admire Schoenberg and his followers but I recognize that the chromatic gamut on which they are based only exists scientifically and that, consequently, the dialectic which is derived from this is artificial.[455]

But Stravinsky wrote about *Pierrot Lunaire:*

> The real wealth of *Pierrot*—sound and substance, for *Pierrot* is the solar plexus as well as the mind of early twentieth-century music—were beyond me as they were beyond all of us at that time, and when Boulez wrote that I had understood it *d'une façon impressioniste*, he was not kind but correct. I *was* aware, nevertheless, that this was the most prescient confrontation in my life.[456]

Alma Mahler (Gustav's wife) once accompanied RAVEL to a concert in Vienna where Schoenberg's Chamber Symphony was performed. Ravel was very nervous throughout the performance. " 'No' he said when we got up at the end, 'that isn't music; that comes out of a laboratory.' "[457]

MESSIAEN recognized that Schoenberg and Berg were the precursors of serial music, but he said that Webern was the "real" serial composer, and for him serial music found its zenith with Pierre Boulez, as he mastered the language and went beyond it instead of being enslaved by it. He admitted that Schoenberg was not a composer he liked more than any other.[458] BOULEZ himself said:

> Cult always kills the man at the centre. Look how repulsive Schoenberg became: "I have discovered a method to save German music". He opened the field but he closed a lot too. The last third of his life was terribly academic. With Opus 25 (the Piano Suite), his work is not attractive anymore. Opus 31 (the Variations for Orchestra) is a lesson in counterpoint and variation. In it he pursues the aesthetic of Brahms. I don't find it interesting to go back to Brahms.[459]

WELLESZ was a pupil of Schoenberg and settled in England in 1939. He wrote a study of Schoenberg that was published in 1971 and included in it this comment:

> Whatever be the attitude of later time towards him, it will be impossible to overlook the fact that it was he who broke through accepted musical conventions which threatened to become mere externalities; that he sacrificed himself, and, by traversing the road of suffering, along with his works which stand as visible monuments of the various stages of his painful career, has given music a new *ethos*, and a sincerity that renounces all that is merely relative and lies outside its own sphere.[460]

A curious commentary about Schoenberg was made by EISLER, who too was a pupil of Schoenberg, but whose Marxist political ideology brought him to regard Schoenberg as a kind of political symbol:

> To the initiated listener Schoenberg's music does not sound beautiful because it mirrors the capitalist world as it is without embellishment and because out of his work the face of capitalism stares directly at us. Due to his genius and complete mastery of technique, this face, revealed so starkly, frightens many. Schoenberg, however, has performed a tremendous historical service. When his music is in the concert halls of the bourgeoisie they are no longer charming and agreeable centres of pleasure where one is moved by one's own beauty but places where one is forced to think about chaos and ugliness of the world or else turn one's face away.[461]

Perhaps we can allow Schoenberg the last word. Once when he was asked if he was the famous composer Arnold Schoenberg, he replied: "No one else wanted the job, so I had to take it on."[462]

Franz Schubert
(1797–1828)

Schubert never met BEETHOVEN face-to-face, although both lived in Vienna at the same time. But Beethoven knew of Schubert and exclaimed once: "Truly in Schubert lives the divine fire!"[463]

SCHUMANN was responsible for discovering Schubert's Symphony in C Major (the *Great*) when he visited Vienna in 1839. When he attended the rehearsals of the symphony in Leipzig under Mendelssohn's direction in the next year, he wrote to Clara Wieck:

> Oh, Clara, I have been in paradise today! They played a symphony of Franz Schubert's. How I wish you had been there, for I cannot describe it to you. The instruments all sing like remarkably intelligent human voices, and the scoring is worthy of Beethoven. Then the length, the heavenly length of it! It is a whole four-volume novel, longer than the choral symphony. I was supremely happy, and had nothing left to wish for, except that you were my wife, and that I could write such symphonies myself.[464]

Schumann also said of the C Major Symphony:

> Deep down in this symphony there lies more than mere song, more than mere joy and sorrow, as already expressed in music in a hundred other instances; it transports us into a world where we cannot recall ever having been before.[465]

He also wrote of the two piano trios of Schubert:

> One glance at Schubert's Trio (op. 99)—and the troubles of our human existence disappear and all the world is fresh and bright again. . . . The

first movement, which in the E flat Trio is eloquent of extreme anger and passionate longing, is here a thing of grace, intimate and virginal; the Adagio, in the E flat Trio a sigh, rising to spiritual anguish, is here a blissful dream-state, a pulsating flow of exquisitely human emotion. The Scherzos are very similar to each other; yet to my mind, that of the B flat Trio is superior. I will not attempt to choose between the two last movements. To sum up, the Trio in E flat is active, masculine, dramatic, while the B flat is passive, feminine, lyrical.[466]

MENDELSSOHN was the conductor of the Leipzig Gewandhaus Orchestra when Schumann heard the C Major Symphony. He described the work in a letter to Moscheles: "We recently played a remarkable and most interesting symphony by Franz Schubert. It is without doubt one of the best works we have lately heard. Throughout bright, fascinating and original, it stands quite at the head of his instrumental works."[467]

MAHLER said after he had read through all of Schubert's chamber music that out of twelve works there will be four, at the most, that are very good. Perhaps eighty of the eight hundred songs are completely beautiful. But all the unimportant works "would almost prompt me, no matter how enthusiastic one was about the rest, to deny his talent."[468]

BRITTEN was a great admirer of Schubert and was one of the finest accompanists in performing his lieder. He said:

It is arguable that the richest and most productive eighteen months in our musical history is the time when Beethoven had just died, when the other nineteenth-century giants, Wagner, Verdi and Brahms had not begun; I mean the period in which Franz Schubert wrote his *Winterreise*, the C Major Symphony, his last three piano sonatas, the C Major Quintet, as well as a dozen other glorious pieces. The very creation of these works in that space of time seems hardly credible; but the standard of inspiration, of magic, is miraculous and past all explanation. Though I have worked very hard at *Winterreise* the last five years, every time I come back to it I am amazed not only by the extraordinary mastery of it—for Schubert knew exactly what he was doing (make no mistake about that), and he had thought profoundly about it—but by the renewal of the magic: each time, the mystery remains.[469]

Robert Schumann (1810–1856)

A considerable music critic himself, Schumann did not appear to be much discussed by his fellow composers. MAHLER said of him:

> Schumann is one of the greatest composers of songs, to be mentioned in the same breath as Schubert. Nobody has mastered the perfected, self-contained form of the Lied as he did. . . . Restrained feeling, true lyricism and profound melancholy pervade his songs of which the dearest to me . . . are those of the *Frauenliebe und -leben* cycle. [470]

GRIEG recognized the equal importance of the piano and the singer in Schumann's songs: "I have no faith in a singer of Schumann's songs who does not appreciate the fact that the piano has quite as great a claim to attention as the singer himself."[471]

SIBELIUS commented about Schumann's four symphonies:

> Construction was not his strong side. And as far as orchestration is concerned there is a certain degree of helplessness. He believed that by doubling with two different instruments (that is, both playing the same notes) he could produce a stronger *forte*. In fact it produces the opposite effect.[472]

BOULEZ compared Schumann to Brahms: "Schumann shows invention where Brahms shows none. Brahms was a banal bourgeois. Schumann, on the contrary, was earlier. He was fresher in his approach."[473]

STRAVINSKY was impressed by one certain aspect of Schumann: "Schumann is *the* composer of childhood, both because he created a child's imaginative world and because children learn some of their first music in his marvellous piano albums."[474]

DELIUS was little interested in the music of what he called the "Immortals." However, he said: "It takes a genius to write a movement like the slow movement in Schumann's Piano Quintet in A Minor, but the third movement is entirely without inspiration."[475]

Alexander Scriabin
(1872–1915)

It was Scriabin's belief that there could be no music per se, and that music could have only one raison d'être, that is to be part of the whole of the *Weltanschauung* (or philosophy of life). He said: "I do not understand how one can write 'mere music'—this is not in itself interesting."[476] His compositions aroused enormous controversy among his fellow composers in Russia. RIMSKY-KORSAKOV'S son said that the *Poem of Ectasy* gave his father "an impression of unhealthy eroticism." Rimsky-Korsakov himself declared after he had heard the work: "He's half out of his mind already."[477] TANEYEV was asked for his impression after hearing one of Scriabin's works; he said: "As if I'd been beaten unmercifully with sticks."[478]

RACHMANINOV, who was an exact contemporary of Scriabin, although he lived much longer, said when he first heard Scriabin's music: "I thought Scriabin was simply a swine, but it seems he is a composer after all."[479] PROKOFIEV heard the *Poem of Ectasy* in 1909 and wrote:

> Both the harmonic and thematic material, and the voice-leading in the counterpoint, were completely new. Basically, Scriabin was trying to find new foundations for harmony. The principle he discovered was very interesting, but in proportion to their complexity they were like a stone tied to Scriabin's neck, hindering his invention as regard melody and (chiefly) the movement of voices. Nonetheless, the *Poem of Ecstasy* was probably his most successful work, since all the elements in his manner of composing were apparently balanced. But it was hard to imagine, at first hearing, just what he was trying to do.

Prokofiev heard the work again shortly after and said:

> Scriabin's orchestration, new in its design, had unfolded before us in all
> the breadth of its sonority. We came away exclaiming "What a genius!"
> But later, when the intellectual coldness of some of Scriabin's "flights"
> became discernible, that opinion had to be downgraded a bit.[480]

ARENSKY wrote in a letter to Taneyev:

> The Russian Symphonic Society played Scriabin's Second Symphony. I
> think there was a gross error in the program: instead of "symphony" they
> should have printed "cacophony", because in this alleged "composition"
> there seems to be a complete absence of all consonance. For thirty or
> forty minutes silence is broken by a continuous series of discords piled
> up one on another without any sense whatever. . . . Rimsky-Korsakov,
> whose opinion I asked, said that he fails to understand how anyone can
> devalue euphony to such an extent.[481]

SHOSTAKOVICH in 1931, when political circumstances in Russia were
somewhat different than in 1909, wrote: "We consider Scriabin as our
bitter musical enemy. Why? Because his music tends toward unhealthy
eroticism. Also to mysticism, passivity and a flight from the reality of
life."[482] STRAVINSKY called Scriabin a "pseudo-esoteric symbolist" and
remarked: "I sometimes think that taste does not matter, but then I listen
to Scriabin."[483]

Dmitry Shostakovich
(1906–1975)

Shostakovich's fellow Soviet composer PROKOFIEV was scathing about him in his public comments:

> He is a talented but somehow "unprincipled" composer and . . . bereft of melodic invention.[484]

> What astonishes me in this [Piano Quintet] is that so young a composer, at the height of his powers, should be so very much on his guard, and so carefully calculate every note. He never takes a single risk. One looks in vain for an impetus, a venture.[485]

STRAVINSKY was usually dismissive of Shostakovich. He described the latter's opera *Lady Macbeth of Mtzensk*, in a letter to Ernest Ansermet after he heard it in 1935 as "formless, monotonous music"[486] and later said of the opera:

> The style of Shostakovich's *Lady Macbeth of Mtzensk* is extremely disturbing, and the score is a work of lamentable provincialism in which the music simply serves as illustration. . . . The music plays a miserable role of illustration, and in an embarrassingly miserable style. Formless, monotonous music. . . . This is not the work of a musician but the product of a total indifference to music in the country of the Soviets.[487]

BRITTEN and Shostakovich developed a close friendship, and Britten gave the first performance outside of the Soviet Union of Shostakovich's Fourteenth Symphony, which was dedicated to him. In 1936 Britten wrote a review of a concert version of *Lady Macbeth of Mtzensk* in which he said: "There is some terrific music in the entr'actes. But I will defend it through thick and thin against these charges of 'lack of style.' . . . There is a consistency of style & method throughout. The satire is biting and brilliant. It is never boring for a second."[488]

Jean Sibelius
(1865–1957)

LAMBERT made an extravagant claim for Sibelius's status as a symphonist: "Not only is Sibelius the most important symphonic writer since Beethoven, but he may even be described as the only writer since Beethoven who has definitely advanced what, after all, is the most complete formal expression of the human spirit."[489] But VIRGIL THOMSON, another composer-critic, did not agree: "I found [the Second Symphony] vulgar, self-indulgent, and provincial beyond all description. I realize that there are sincere Sibelius-lovers in the world, though I must say I've never met one among educated professional musicians."[490]

Sibelius had other champions. RICHARD STRAUSS wrote in his diary: "Sibelius is the only Scandinavian composer who has real depth. Though he lacks a total mastery of instrumentation, his music has a freshness that presupposes a virtually inexhaustible fund of melodic invention."[491] RAVEL, too: "A magnificent talent—I do not say a supreme artist, but a composer strong in feeling and color and inspired by his vast and sombre north."[492]

Stravinsky recalled having once heard Sibelius's First and Second Symphonies with RIMSKY-KORSAKOV, whose only comment was: "I suppose that is also possible."[493] IVES was scathing:

> The *Valse Triste* (as brown-sugar-coddle as it is) is bigger than what [we] heard last night—but these symphonies, overtures etc. are worse because they give out the strut of little music making believe it's big. Every phrase, line, and chord, and beat went over and over the way you'd exactly expect it would—trite, tiresome awnings of platitudes, all a nice mixture of Grieg, Wagner and Tchaikovsky (et al, ladies).[494]

Johann Strauss
(1825–1899)

"Brahms is the spirit of Vienna," said MASSENET, "Strauss is the perfume."[495] The waltzes and other music of Johann Strauss were much loved by many composers of more serious vein. BRAHMS never missed a performance of *Die Fledermaus*; his admiration for Strauss was genuine, and on one occasion at a social gathering where musical friends of Madame Johann Strauss were writing their names on her fan with phrases from their works, Brahms wrote the opening measures of *The Beautiful Blue Danube* waltz, and underneath it, "*Not*, I regret to say, by your devoted friend, Johannes Brahms."[496]

RICHARD STRAUSS (who was not a relative of Johann Strauss) paid tribute to the "natural talent" of the latter. In an age "where all about him had already turned towards the complex and the premeditated, [he] was one of the last to have primary inspirations."[497] At another time he referred to him as a composer of genius, and in his first season as conductor at the Berlin Court Opera he gave the first performance there of *Die Fledermaus*.

MAHLER said: "I certainly don't hold a low opinion of the waltzes; I accept them for what they are, in all their uniqueness and delightful inventiveness."[498] But Mahler also pointed out that absolutely nothing develops from the short melodies each of eight-bar phrases, and they cannot be called "compositions in any sense of the word." He compared them to Schubert's *Moments Musicaux*, where the development of each single bar is a work of art.[499]

Richard Strauss
(1864–1949)

Strauss's fellow composers certainly reacted to him in different ways. TCHAIKOVSKY, for example, said: "Such an astounding lack of talent has never before been united to such pretentiousness."[500] MAHLER remarked: "I don't know myself what to make of Strauss. How is one to explain his unequalness and jumbling together of good and bad?"[501] He also said: "Strauss and I tunnel from the opposite sides of the mountain. One day we shall meet."[502] ELGAR was more sympathetic: "Strauss is the greatest genius of the age, and his later works I like best of all, much distinguished opinion to the contrary notwithstanding. His *Don Juan* is the greatest masterpiece of the present, and his *Heldenleben* and *Zarathustra* I find almost as inspiring."[503]

RAVEL always said how much he had learnt about orchestration by reading the scores of Rimsky-Korsakov and Strauss. He used to say: "Strauss is the liberator who was able to extend the liberties taken by Berlioz, and he has given the wind instruments a new importance, new at least for the time when he was writing."[504] Nevertheless Ravel added, particularly with *Till Eulenspiegel* in mind, that despite his complete admiration for Strauss's skill as an orchestrator, "It's only his irresistible comic sense which sometimes saves his tunes from an excessive facile sentimentality."[505]

Discussing Strauss's symphonic poems, COPLAND concluded:

> Despite obvious weaknesses . . . they are remarkable achievements. As pictorial representation they have few rivals, and as treatment of forms that were free they were the first of their kind. . . . In *Ein Heldenleben* or *Also sprach Zarathustra*, where the form may be said to be sectionally built, the mere size is so big as to make the composition dangerously top-

heavy. It is a question whether the human mind can really relate the separate moments of a free form that lasts for more than forty minutes without pause. That, at any rate, is what Strauss asks us to do.[506]

DEBUSSY described Strauss's music as a book of pictures, even moving pictures, saying that he thought in colored images.[507] Debussy detected elements of Berlioz and Liszt in Strauss, but none of Wagner. *Tod und Verklärung*, he wrote, could not conceal the innate vulgarity of certain of its themes.[508] He called *Till Eulenspiegel* "an hour of the new music played to lunatics," although he could not deny a genius at work, especially in the amazing assurance of the orchestral writing and the "wild sense of movement that sweeps us along from beginning to end, compelling us to share in each of the hero's merry pranks."[509]

BARTÓK was astonished at the classical simplicity of the *Sinfonia domestica,* as well as its complete lack of cacophony; the entire work could pass as a work of absolute music, ideally blending unity and variety.[510] He said that Strauss's first works showed the influence of Brahms, but after he came under the influence of Wagner and Liszt and began to write symphonic poems, a new impulse showed itself in his music.[511] Bartók preferred *Salome* to *Elektra*; *Elektra* to him was average Strauss, without an idea that would stimulate him to read or hear it a second time. He said that he did not understand how someone so gifted could write such flat "half-hearted" music in his operas or other works when "so-called sublime feelings are expressed."[512]

On the contrary, STRAVINSKY thought *Elektra* surpassed *Salome*: "[*Elektra*] is Strauss's best composition. Let them talk about the vulgarisms that are always present in Strauss—to which my reply is that the more deeply one goes into German works of art, the more one sees that *all* of them suffer from that. . . . Strauss's *Elektra* is a marvellous thing!"[513]

Others were enthusiastic about *Salome*. RACHMANINOV saw the opera in Dresden and wrote that he was delighted with it, "most of all the orchestra, of course, but there are many things in the music . . . whenever it didn't sound too discordant."[514] MAHLER wrote to Strauss about *Salome*:

> I cannot help speaking of the moving impression your work made on me when I read it recently! This is your apogee so far! Indeed, I assert that *nothing* that even you have done up to now can be compared to it. You know—I don't go in for empty phrases. With you even less than with others. Every note is right! What I have long known: you are a natural dramatist! I confess that it is only through your music that Wilde's work has become comprehensible to me.[515]

In 1947 Strauss visited London. During the rehearsal for the concert when Norman Del Mar conducted a fantasia on *Die Frau ohne Schatten*,

Strauss went to the conductor's desk, looked glumly at the score for a few moments, muttered "All my own fault," and went away. Later during his visit he conducted the Philharmonia Orchestra himself, and before going onto the podium he said: "So the old horse ambles out of the stables once more!" At a rehearsal for one of these concerts he said to the orchestra: "No, I know what I want, and I know what I meant when I wrote this. After all, I may not be a first-rate composer, but I *am* a first-class second-rate composer."[516]

Igor Stravinsky
(1882–1971)

BERNSTEIN summed up the life and music of Stravinsky:

> In his long and abundantly creative life, Stravinsky produced a highly
> personal body of work which seems to sum up all of music itself—from
> primitive folk art to highly sophisticated serialism, from rarified church
> music to outspoken jazz. . . . Through some private alchemy, some secret
> magic, he absorbed all these essences, metamorphosed them, and gave
> them back to us shiny-new, original, inimitable.[517]

DUKAS commented in 1923: "Every single one of his works reveals a
new and unprecedented Stravinsky. And every single one of his works
seems to invent its own rule, which springs from its conception and applies
to that work alone. So much so that with Stravinksy the expression confirms
the exception."[518]

Going back to Stravinsky's student days in St. Petersburg, one of his
teachers, GLAZUNOV, said: "Of all the two thousand pupils I taught at
the conservatory in St. Petersburg [Stravinsky] had the worst ear."[519] It is
said that the student Stravinsky took a new composition to another of his
teachers, RIMSKY-KORSAKOV, who said to him: "This is disgusting,
Sir. No Sir, it is not permissible to write such nonsense until one is sixty."[520]

SHOSTAKOVICH said: "Stravinsky is the only composer of our century
whom I would call great without any doubt."[521] He added: "Fools think
that Stravinsky's composing deteriorated towards the end. . . . To my taste,
it's just the reverse. It's the early works that I like less—for instance, *The
Rite of Spring*, which is rather crude, so much of it calculated for external
effect and lacking substance."[522]

EISLER, the German composer with Marxist convictions, saw Stravinsky in a different light when he wrote this in 1948:

> If Schoenberg is an isolated intellectual, Stravinsky is the "gentleman", completely at ease in the modern milieu. Stravinsky's neo-classical style is cautious, smart, cold, open, constricted and imitative. The main features of neo-classicism are impassiveness, the imperviousness of the artist to the object that he presents, coldness, a fixed manner of ornamentation, mechanical configuration, quotations from pre-Beethoven melismata, lack of motivation, the static, the non-symphonic, the shortness of forms. . . . Neo-classicism is a phenomenon of the big bourgeoisie. It is arrogant and cold to the man in the street; it is the musical side of "good society."[523]

BARTÓK defended Stravinsky's use of themes from other composers' music and other sources:

> Stravinsky never mentions the sources of his themes. . . . [He] apparently takes this course deliberately. He wants to demonstrate that it does not matter a jot whether a composer invents his own themes or uses themes from elsewhere. He has a right to use musical material taken from all sources. . . . In maintaining that the question of the origin of a theme is completely unimportant from the artist's point of view, Stravinsky is right. The question of origin can only be interesting from the point of view of musical documentation.[524]

BLITZSTEIN considered Stravinsky just short of true greatness:

> Stravinsky's greatness is the greatness of C.P.E. Bach. . . . Several of his works approach the final greatness of Mozart, of Monteverdi, of J. S. Bach. They have conceptions and an initial impulse of comparable size; they are important utterances. But something intervenes to make them less than crucial masterpieces—some powerful flaw, subtle or obvious, spoiling part or all of the work. In *Oedipus Rex* two scenes go under, carrying with them the basic security of all the rest; yet the psychological content of *Oedipus* is among the most momentous in music. In the *Sacre du printemps* the fragment-scheme gets beyond the composer's control, resulting in a form that is little better than a high-class medley. In the *Symphonie de Psaumes* a fundamental confusion exists between what is spiritually and what is sensually compelling. There is no denying the greatness of Stravinsky. It is just that he is not great enough.[525]

MESSIAEN saw great significance in *Le Sacre du printemps*:

> Stravinsky is of immense importance because he was the first to replace the accent on *Rhythm*: by the use of solely rhythmic themes, superimposed rhythmic ostinati, and above all in creating (consciously or unconsciously) the process of "rhythmic characters". This last process follows, by am-

plifying it, the Beethovenian type of development or "development by elimination". *The Glorification of the Chosen One* and even more the *Ritual Dance* of *The Rite of Spring* are striking examples of juxtaposition and movements by augmentation, diminution or immobility of "rhythmic characters."[526]

LAMBERT wrote of *Le Sacre*: "A work which was merely the logical outcome of a barbaric outlook applied to the technique of impressionism."[527] DEBUSSY'S opinion of *Le Sacre* was that it "is an extraordinarily savage affair.... If you like, it is primitive with every modern convenience." Talking at the time of World War I, he said: "It seems to me that Stravinsky is trying to make music with non-musical means in the same way as the Germans are now pretending to produce steak out of sawdust."[528] Writing to Stravinsky, Debussy praised *Petrushka*, finding in it an orchestral infallibility that he had found only in *Parsifal*. He felt that Stravinsky could be proud of his achievement in the work, which possessed a kind of sonorous magic where mechanical souls became human by a spell of which Stravinsky seemed to be the unique inventor.[529]

PROKOFIEV was critical of Stravinsky's first three great ballets. "What vivid, almost blinding colors in the score, what inventiveness in all these grimaces and how sincere the creation," he said of *The Firebird*, "but I could not for a moment be captivated by the music. Where is the music? Nothing but dead wood." Of *Petrushka*: "Stravinsky, in the most interesting moments, in the most vivid scenes, does not write music, but something that illustrates this or that action exceptionally well.... If he cannot write music for the most important parts of the scenario but fills them in with any old stuff, then this indeed shows his musical limitations."[530] After he heard *Le Sacre du printemps*, he remarked: "I understood nothing of it at all."[531]

DELIUS obviously had no sympathy for Stravinsky, saying that "Grieg had more music in his little finger than Stravinsky has in his whole body."[532] Poulenc recorded that RAVEL did not like any of Stravinsky's music from *Les Noces* onwards. Ravel himself said that Stravinsky could "take liberties I could not allow myself because he is less of a musician than I am."[533]

SCHOENBERG was unimpressed with *Oedipus Rex*:

I do not know what I am supposed to like in *Oedipus*. At least, it is all negative: unusual theatre, unusual setting, unusual resolution of the action, unusual vocal writing, unusual acting, unusual melody, unusual harmony, unusual counterpoint, unusual instrumentation—all this "un", without *being* anything in particular. I could say that all Stravinsky has composed is the dislike his work is meant to inspire.[534]

Reconsidering his remarks later, Schoenberg wrote: "I still believe this work is nothing—even though I really liked *Petrushka*. Parts of it very much indeed."[535]

The young BRITTEN wrote in his diary after an early performance of *Oedipus Rex* in 1936:

> One of the peaks of Stravinsky's output, this work shows his wonderful sense of style and power of drawing inspiration from every age of music, and leaving the whole a perfect shape, satisfying every aesthetic demand. And, of course, the established idea of originality dies so hard, it is easy to see why the later works of Stravinsky are regarded with such disfavour.[536]

Finally, here is Stravinsky's response to his critics: "The critics cannot judge me. Not only am I more important in music, but I *know* more than they do."[537]

Sergey Taneyev
(1856–1915)

The pianist, conductor, composer, and teacher Taneyev was very influential in Russia, but his compositions are little known elsewhere. RACHMAN-INOV wrote this tribute to Taneyev:

> For all of us who knew him and sought him out, he was the finest judge, possessing wisdom, a sense of justice, affability and simplicity. He was a model in everything, in his every act, for everything he did he only did well. Through his personal example he taught us how to live, how to think, how to work, even how to speak, for he spoke in a particularly Taneyev way: concisely, clearly and to the point.[538]

Peter Tchaikovsky
(1840–1893)

Although there have been published many comments by Tchaikovsky about other composers, taken mostly from his letters, there appears to be much less about him in the known remarks of others. One who admired him and said so was STRAVINSKY, who stated that he was "one of the few Russian composers of whom I am really fond."[539] Stravinsky defended Tchaikovsky against the charge of "vulgarity":

> It seems to me that to be "vulgar" is not to be in one's proper place, and surely Tchaikovsky's art, devoid as it is of all pretentiousness, cannot be accused of this fault. . . . The "pathos" of his music is a part of his nature, not the pretension of an artistic ideal.[540]

Stravinsky also identified the specifically Russian character of the ballet, *The Sleeping Beauty*, his remarks appearing in a letter he wrote to *The Times* in London in 1921:

> Tchaikovsky's music . . . is often more profoundly Russian than music which has long since been awarded the facile label of Muscovite picturesqueness. This music is quite as Russian as Pushkin's verse or Glinka's song. While not specifically cultivating in his art the "soul of the Russian peasant", Tchaikovsky drew *unconsciously* from the true popular sources of our race.[541]

Stravinsky agreed with PROKOFIEV that *Eugen Onegin* is the most Russian opera of all: "Not only because every young Russian woman has something of Tatyana, and in some way dreams of being a Tatyana, but also from the beginning to the end the atmosphere is intrinsically Russian!"[542] PROKOFIEV added that Tchaikovsky "is certainly our greatest opera composer."[543]

TANEYEV was critical of Tchaikovsky's Fourth Symphony:

> Exceedingly nice. . . . The scherzo is marvellous, and sounds excellent; I don't like the trio which is like a dance out of a ballet. . . . One of this symphony's failings with which I shall never be able to reconcile myself is that in each movement there is something that recalls ballet music: the middle of the Andante, the trio of the scherzo, the march-like bit in the finale. . . . That's my *honest* opinion of this symphony.[544]

MAHLER was certainly not charmed by the Sixth Symphony, the *Pathétique*:

> A shallow, superficial, distressingly homophonic work—no better than salon music. Even coloring should not really be the sort of thing he gives us here. He is fake, sand thrown in one's eyes! If you look more closely, these meaningless sequences of chords can't disguise the fundamental lack of invention and the emptiness.[545]

Giuseppe Verdi
(1813–1901)

The great forerunner of Verdi as composer of Italian opera, ROSSINI, said in the year of his death: "Verdi is a composer whose character is melancholy and serious; his sadness reflects his true nature. I esteem him greatly."[546] On another, earlier, occasion, Rossini said: "I like very much [Verdi's] almost savage nature, not to mention his great power of expressing his passions."[547]

BRAHMS once heard the conductor Hans von Bülow speaking in disparaging terms of Verdi's *Requiem*. He went immediately to a music store, bought the score and read it through, and, when he had finished, said: "Bülow has made a fool of himself for all time: only a genius could have written that."[548]

BIZET, whose *Carmen* rivals the best operas of Verdi in popularity, wrote:

> Verdi is a man of great talent who lacks the essential quality that makes *great masters*: style. But he has marvellous bursts of passion. His passion is brutal, it is true, but it is better to be passionate that way than not at all. His music is sometimes exasperating, but never boring. All in all, I understand neither the idolizers nor the detractors he has aroused. To my mind, he merits neither the one nor the other.[549]

Bizet also offered this assessment after attending the première of *Don Carlos*:

Don Carlos is *very* bad. I adore *Traviata* and *Rigoletto*. *Don Carlos* is a sort of compromise. No melody, no accent. It aims at a style, but only aims.... It was a complete, absolute *failure*.[550]

WAGNER all but ignored Verdi. It was not until the twentieth century that other composers generally came to recognize his genius. STRAVINSKY said:

The great mighty Verdi. How many beautiful things there are in his early works as well as the final ones. I admire him unconditionally, a truly great composer! I prefer Verdi to all other music of the nineteenth century.[551]

VAUGHAN WILLIAMS wrote in his musical autobiography:

I heard Verdi's *Requiem* for the first time. At first I was properly shocked by the frank sentimentalism and sensationalism of the music. I remember being particularly horrified at the drop of a semitone on the word "Dona". Was this not the purest "village organist"? But in a very few minutes the music possessed me. I realized that here was a composer who could do all the things which I, with my youthful pedantry, thought wrong—indeed, would be unbearable in a lesser man; music which was sentimental, theatrical, occasionally even cheap, and yet was an overpowering masterpiece.[552]

BRITTEN made this assessment of Verdi:

Verdi can, of course, write the obvious square tunes, which use many repetitions of the same little phrase and work to an effective climax. These abound in the early operas, and are immediately endearing.... But he can also write the long casual lines, a succession of apparently unrelated phrases, which repeated hearings discover to have an enormous tension below the surface.... Verdi has the gift, which only the greatest have had: that of writing a succession of the simplest harmonies in such a way as to sound surprising and yet "right."... Then later in his life he developed a new kind of harmonic originality, which I can most easily describe by reminding the reader of the astounding string accompaniment to the bell strokes in the last scene of *Falstaff*.... His attitude to the voices on the stage and the orchestra. This seems to me to be perfectly right. The voices dominate, and the orchestra in the background—but what a background!... In the construction of his later works Verdi seems to have discovered the secret of perfection. At the beginning of his life he accepted the convention of the times in the sharp definition of the numbers, and he balanced those numbers brilliantly. Fundamentally, he never changed this attitude, but later on the numbers melt into each other with a really astonishing subtlety.... I have no space to write about his vitality, his breadth of humanity, his courage, his extraordinary career which developed into an almost divine serenity. . . . I am an arrogant and impatient listener, but in the case of few composers, a very few, when I hear a work I do not like I am convinced it is my own fault. Verdi is one of these composers.[553]

Richard Wagner
(1813–1883)

Wagner himself wrote much about his historical role in music, especially in the evolution of opera. He aroused adulation in many of his contemporaries, but he ignored some composers, such as Brahms, and Verdi, who today are regarded as scarcely less important than himself by the musical public.

Wagner met BERLIOZ in Paris in 1860 and sent him the score of *Tristan und Isolde.* Berlioz wrote: "I have read and re-read this strange piece of music; I have listened to it with the profoundest attention and lively desire to discover the sense of it; well, I have to admit that I still haven't the least notion of what the composer is driving at."[554]

There are many stories about what ROSSINI said about Wagner. He was asked how he liked the performance of *Tannhäuser*; he answered, with a satirical smile, "It is music one must hear several times. I am not going again."[555] Rossini also said: "Mr. Wagner has beautiful moments, but bad quarters of an hour."[556] A friend once found him studying the score of *Tristan und Isolde* and asked him what he thought of it. "Ah," he said, "It is a beautiful work! I never expected to find such grace of expression, such power of invention in the music of the reformer of our old dramatic operas, the scores of Mozart, Gluck, Cimarosa, Weber, Mercadante, Meyerbeer—and my own!" His visitor, coming closer, was dumbfounded to observe that Rossini was reading Wagner's score upside down. Whereupon, inverting the score, Rossini said after a glance, "Alas, now I cannot make head or tail of it!"[557]

During one of his weekly dinners for which Rossini brought together some noted guests, at the point at which the menu mentioned *turbot à l'allemande*, the servants placed before the guests a very appetizing sauce, of which each took his portion. Then nothing else was served. The turbot did not appear. The guests, perplexed, asked one another, "What does one do with this sauce?" Then Rossini, maliciously enjoying their embarrassment, and himself gulping down the sauce said, "And so, you are still waiting for something? Enjoy the sauce; believe me, it is excellent. As for the turbot—alas! the principal dish . . . it is just . . . the fisherman forgot at the last moment to bring it; don't be astonished! Isn't it the same with Wagner's music? . . . Good sauce, but no turbot! . . . no melody!"[558]

SCHUMANN lived in Dresden at the same time as Wagner, whom he met occasionally. Schumann said that Wagner had "the most amazing gift of the gab, and is always chock full of his own ideas; one cannot listen to him for long."[559] He did not think much of Wagner as a conductor, either: "How is it possible for an orchestra to produce a perfect performance, when the conductor himself does not understand the work?"[560] After reading the score of *Tannhäuser*, Schumann wrote to Mendelssohn:

> There is Wagner, who has just finished another opera, undoubtedly a clever fellow, full of crazy ideas and bold to degree. . . . I declare he cannot write or imagine four consecutive bars that are melodious, or *even correct*. That is what they all lack—pure harmony and capacity for four-part choral composition. . . . The music is not a shade better than *Rienzi*; in fact, rather weaker and more strained.[561]

But after he saw a stage performance of the opera, he changed his mind and acknowledged the work's power. Later he wrote of "a mysterious magic that overpowers our senses" in Wagner's operas.[562]

TCHAIKOVSKY was not converted to Wagner. He summed up his opinion:

> In spite of his great creative gifts, in spite of his talents as a poet, and his extensive culture, Wagner's services to art—and to opera in particular—have been of a negative kind. . . . To compel people to listen for four hours at a stretch to an endless symphony which, however rich in orchestral color, is wanting in clearness and directness of thought; to keep singers all these long hours singing melodies which have no independent existence, but are merely notes that belong to this symphonic music . . . this is certainly not the ideal to which contemporary musicians should aim. . . . As regards the dramatic interest of his operas, I find them very poor, often childishly naive.[563]

VERDI, who was one of Wagner's greatest admirers, said:

> He is one of the greatest geniuses. . . . I never cease exploring [his] sublime world of ideas.
> The work which arouses my greatest admiration is *Tristan*. The giant

structure fills me time and time again with astonishment and awe, and I still cannot quite comprehend that it was conceived and written by a human being. I consider the second act, in its wealth of musical invention, its tenderness and sensuality of musical expression and its inspired orchestration, to be one of the finest creations that has ever issued from a human mind.[564]

Wagner was generally dismissive of BRAHMS, but Brahms himself had many a good word to say about Wagner. One of Brahms's most intimate friends was Clara Schumann, and he once wrote to her, saying: "I am not enthusiastic . . . about Wagner in general, but I listen as attentively as possible, that is, for as long as I can stand it."[565] At the same time Brahms is described as having called Wagner's music dramas "great works, so ideally conceived and executed."[566] Brahms called himself "the best of Wagnerites" and rejoiced in the honors showered on Wagner, believing that the position of every musician had been raised by them. The Viennese critic Eduard Hanslick stated that Brahms's comprehension of Wagner's scores was probably more profound than that of any other man, apart from Wagner, and that he often heard Brahms defend Wagner against hostile critics. Of the four operas of *The Ring*, Brahms said that *Die Walküre* and *Götterdämmerung* had a "great hold" on him, but he did not particularly care for *Rheingold* and *Siegfried*. Of *Siegfried* he said: "I am sure nobody would see anything particular in it if one of us had written it . . . and those endless duets!"[567] Of *Tristan und Isolde* he said: "If I look at [the score] in the morning, I am cross for the rest of the day."[568]

CUI wrote in a letter to Rimsky-Korsakov:

Wagner is a man devoid of all talent. His melodies, where they are found at all, are in worse taste than Verdi and Flotow and more sour than the stalest Mendelssohn. All this is covered up with a thick layer of rot. His orchestra is decorative, but coarse. The violins squeal throughout on the highest notes and throw the listener into a state of extreme nervousness. I left without waiting for the concert to end, and I assure you that had I stayed longer, both I and my wife would have had a fit of hysterics. What nerves must Wagner himself possess?[569]

Of *The Ring* DEBUSSY wrote:

It is difficult to imagine the effect made even on the toughest mind by the four evenings of *The Ring*. One is more than obsessed; one is subjugated. . . . Normal civilised behaviour cannot henceforth prevent us from greeting our fellow creatures with cries of the Valkyries: "Hohjotoho! Hoioha! Hoioha! Hoiho!"[570]

But Debussy had the highest praise for the music itself:

Suddenly, effects loom up of unforgettable beauty. They are as irresistible as the sea. . . . One does not criticise a work of such magnitude as the Ring. . . . Its too sumptuous greatness renders futile the legitimate desire to grasp its proportions.[571]

D'INDY'S assessment of Wagner's influence is perceptive:

In all music, as in nature, there are mountains and valleys; there are artists of genius who raise their art to such great heights that the herd of second-rate creators, unable to breathe in these altitudes, is forced to descend again to more temperate levels (which, however, are often sown with charming flowers) until the eruption of new genius heaves up some new mountain peak.

Such were Bach, Haydn, Beethoven and César Franck in the symphonic order; and in the dramatic order, Palestrina, Monteverdi, Rameau, Gluck and Wagner. At the present moment we are descending the slope created by the Wagnerian upheaval, and we are hastening gently towards the hopeful presage of a new summit. But all our drama—even that of composers who most energetically deny the imputation—comes from the spring which rises at the feet of the titanic Wagner.

Richard Wagner casts his great shadow over all our musico-dramatic production. But it is certain that the latent work that is going on in the souls of creative artists is to favour the ascent towards a distant height, of which we cannot yet foresee either the glaciers or the precipices.[572]

M. D. Calvocoressi, who knew RAVEL, said that there was little that Ravel could admire in Wagner's music, but that little he admired very greatly.[573] POULENC said that after listening to an opera of Wagner he felt the need "to cleanse his spirit and his ears" by listening to Mozart.[574] MASSENET said: "So overwhelming is the power of Wagner that after hearing one of his works one vows never to compose another thing. Afterwards one forgets a little and begins again."[575]

MAHLER said: "When my spirits are low I have only to think of Wagner and my mood improves. How amazing that a light like his ever penetrated the world! . . . But then he was born at the right moment, at the precise juncture of time when the world was waiting for what he had to say and offer."[576] Mahler once remarked that "Rienzi was Wagner's most beautiful opera and the greatest musical drama ever composed."[577] Of Die Meistersinger he said: "If the whole of German art were to disappear, it could be recognised and reconstructed from this one work."[578]

RICHARD STRAUSS too admired Die Meistersinger, writing in a letter to Hugo von Hofmannsthal:

Wagner tells in his autobiography in unforgettable detail how much it was Nuremberg, to what great extent it was his discovery and perception of

German life and manners in this city world which gave him the germ for *Meistersinger*. Even the night-time street brawl and the watchman who marks the transition to a tranquil mood have their place in this truly poetic personal experience. This is what gives the opera its indestructible truth: that it brings to life again a genuine, complete world which did exist— not like *Lohengrin* and *Tannhäuser* or even the *Ring* (*Tristan* is a different matter altogether) imaginary or excogitated worlds which have never existed anywhere. . . . This is what makes it so firm and solid and un-ageing.[579]

RIMSKY-KORSAKOV and GLAZUNOV attended rehearsals of *The Ring* conducted by Karl Muck in St. Petersburg. Rimsky-Korsakov said afterwards: "Wagner's handling of the orchestra astonished both of us, and from this time onward Wagner's methods gradually permeated our orchestral writing."[580] He also wrote on another occasion: "What terrible harm Wagner did by interspersing his pages of genius with harmonic and modulatory outrages."[581] Shostakovich said that Glazunov liked to recount how he "penetrated" Wagner:

I listened to *Die Walküre* the first time, understood absolutely nothing, and didn't like it at all. I went a second time. Nothing again. And a third time—the same. How many times do you think I went to hear that opera before I understood it? Nine times. On the tenth, finally, I understood it. And I liked it very much.[582]

SIBELIUS wrote after hearing *Tristan und Isolde*: "Nothing, not even *Parsifal* made as overwhelming an impression. It leaves one feeling that everything else is pale and feeble by comparison." But at another time he said: "Wagner is gross, brutal, vulgar and totally lacking with fine feelings. For example, he will shout 'I love you, I love you etc . . .' in my view this is something that should be whispered."[583]

After hearing *Tristan und Isolde,* NIELSEN wrote in his diary:

Wagner's characters undertake too little; they only talk. They talk about what has happened, what's happening, and what is going to happen. Yet nothing happens at all. These human beings cannot act, and Wagner neither. As a dramatic poet he is nothing and as a dramatic composer almost nothing; as soon as he tries to express life and passionate emotions they become tawdry. As a lyric poet he is great, but with lyrics one does not construct a drama; they melt away.[584]

STRAVINSKY saw *Parsifal* at Bayreuth and was not impressed:

What I find revolting in the whole affair is the underlying conception which dictated it—the principle of putting a work of art on the same level as the sacred and symbolic ritual which institutes a religious service. And, indeed, is not all this comedy of Bayreuth, with its ridiculous formalities, simply an unconscious aping of a religious rite?[585]

We give the last word to Debussy: "Wagner was a beautiful sunset that was mistaken for a dawn."[586]

Carl Maria Von Weber
(1786–1826)

Weber's opera *Der Freischütz* is one of the cornerstones of German Romantic music. BEETHOVEN admired it:

> I never would have thought it of the gentle little man. Now Weber must write operas; nothing but operas—one after the other and without polishing them too much. Casper, the monster, stands out like a house. Wherever the devil puts in his claws they are felt.[587]

BERLIOZ too:

> The poetic invention of [*Der Freischütz*] . . . is full of energy, passion and contrast; the supernatural element in it gives rise to strange and startling effects. Melody, harmony and rhythm alike are tremendously vivid and powerful; everything combines to arouse the listener. In addition the characters, being drawn from life, are more obviously appealing; the representation of the feelings and the world they live in has naturally prompted a less rarified, more accessible style [than *Oberon*]; yet it is treated with such exquisite skill that the most austere spirit cannot resist its charm, while for the same quality the mass of the people deem it the very perfection of art and a miracle of invention.[588]

SCHUMANN admired *Euryanthe:* "The music is as yet far too little known and recognised. It is heart's blood, the noblest he had; the opera cost him part of his life—truly. But it has also made him immortal."[589]
DEBUSSY marvelled at the horn call at the opening of *Oberon*, saying that "only in *Parsifal* is there anything comparable to the eternal youthfulness of *Oberon* and *Der Freischütz*."[590] ROSSINI'S opinion of Weber

was much less complimentary; Berlioz recorded him as saying that Weber's music gave him the colic.[591] NIELSEN, too, is a dissenting voice:

> I've come to the conclusion that Weber will be forgotten in a hundred year's [sic] time. There is something jelly-like about a lot of his things. It is a fact that he who brandishes the hardest fist will be remembered longest. Beethoven, Michelangelo, Bach, Berlioz, Rembrandt, Shakespeare, Goethe, Ibsen and the like have all given their time a black eye.[592]

One close to RAVEL has written that Weber was one of his really favorite composers, and his admiration for him kept growing until the end of his life. "How many times had I heard him extolling the merits of *Der Freischütz?* . . . He used to claim that, without Weber, Wagner would not perhaps have achieved the initimate communion between text and music."[593]

Anton Von Webern
(1883–1945)

A student of Arnold Schoenberg and a founder with him and Alban Berg
of the Second Viennese School, Webern is noted, for one thing, for the
brevity of his music. In the foreword to Webern's Six Bagatelles for String
Quartet, Op. 9, SCHOENBERG wrote:

> While the brevity of these pieces is their eloquent advocate, such brevity
> stands equally in need of advocacy. Think what self-denial it takes to cut
> a long story so short. A glance can always be spun out into a poem, a
> sigh into a novel. But to convey a novel through a single gesture, or felicity
> by a single catch of the breath: such concentration exists only when emo-
> tional self-indulgence is correspondingly absent.[594]

BOULEZ, one of the most important interpreters of Webern's music,
said:

> Webern's vocabulary attracted me at the start. I found it very important
> because it established a grammatic base. But I find that the more Webern
> went on, the more simple his forms became—too simple, in fact, for my
> taste. One hearing alone is sufficient to catch the essence of his vocabulary.
> One does not need a series of readings. It's like a painting of Mondrian.
> You see the perfection right away and it is very striking, but when you
> return to it, there is nothing more to take. That is very different from
> Cézanne, whose paintings I can look at over and over again because of
> their complexity, because of the infinite detail in design and texture. In
> that sense Cézanne can be compared to Berg.[595]

Subsequently Boulez concluded: "Webern thirty years later is a historical quantity, solidified lava, no longer something directly vital to me."[596]

STRAVINSKY wrote beautifully about Webern ten years after his death in 1945:

> The 15th of September 1945, the day of Webern's death, should be a day of mourning for any receptive musician. We must hail not only this great composer but also a real hero. Doomed to a total failure in a deaf world of ignorance and indifference he inexorably kept on cutting out his diamonds, his dazzling diamonds, the mines of which he had such perfect knowledge.[597]

In conclusion, BRITTEN'S assessment: "Very fresh and cleansing, but the baby seems to have gone out with the bathwater."[598]

Hugo Wolf
(1860–1903)

Wolf, one of the great German lied writers in the nineteenth century, is reported to have said:

> I sent [BRAHMS] a song five years ago and asked him to mark a cross in the score wherever he thought it was faulty. He sent it back unread, saying: "I don't want to make a cemetery of your composition."[599]

Notes and Sources

1. Karl Geiringer, *Haydn: A Creative Life in Music* (London: Allen & Unwin, 1947), 40–41.

2. *The Beethoven Companion*, ed. Denis Arnold and Nigel Fortune (London: Faber, 1971), 142.

3. Malcolm Boyd, *Bach* (London: Dent, 1983), 218.

4. *The Letters of Mozart and His Family*, ed. Emily Anderson, 3d ed. (London, Macmillan, 1985), 801.

5. Alexander Wheelock Thayer, *Life of Beethoven* (Princeton: Princeton University Press, 1967), 956.

6. "Sayings of Beethoven," *Musical Quarterly* 13 (1927): 202.

7. Ibid., 201.

8. *Felix Mendelssohn: Letters,* ed. G. Selden-Goth (New York: Vienna House, 1973), 34.

9. Ibid., 240.

10. Ibid., 201.

11. Ronald Taylor, *Robert Schumann: His Life and Work* (London, Granada, 1982), 71.

12. Ibid.

13. Herbert Weinstock, *Rossini: A Biography* (London: Oxford University Press, 1968), 264.

14. *Figaro*, 19 October 1891, quoted in *The Music Lover's Miscellany*, ed. Eric Blom (London: Gollancz, 1935), 89.

15. *Cosima Wagner's Diaries*, trans. Geoffrey Skelton, vol. 1 (London, Collins, 1978), 164.

16. Florence May, *The Life of Johannes Brahms* (London, 1905), quoted in *The Book of Musical Anecdotes*, ed. Norman Lebrecht (London: Andre Deutsch, 1985), 204–5.

17. Natalie Bauer-Lechner, *Recollections of Gustav Mahler,* trans. Dika Newlin (London: Faber, 1980), 166.

18. Ibid., 169–70.

19. Ibid.

20. *The New Music Lover's Handbook*, ed. Elie Siegmeister (New York: Harvey House, 1973), frontispiece.

21. Breitkopf & Härtel catalogue of the works of Johann Sebastian Bach, 1909, preface.

22. Igor Stravinsky, *Poetics of Music* (New York: Vintage, 1956), 135.

23. Igor Stravinsky and Robert Craft, *Retrospectives and Conclusions* (New York: Knopf, 1969), 65.

24. Claude Samuel, *Conversations with Olivier Messiaen*, trans. Felix Aprahamian (London: Stainer & Bell, 1976), 26.

25. Nikolay Rimsky-Korsakov, *Record of My Musical Life* (Moscow, 1955), 18.

26. Edward Garden, *Balakirev* (London: Faber, 1966), 82–3.

27. Ibid., 90.

28. Letter from Tchaikovsky to Madame von Meck, 1877, quoted in Edward Garden, *Balakirev* (London: Faber, 1966), 15.

29. László Eösze, *Zoltán Kodály: His Life and Work*, trans. István Farkas and Gyula Gulyás (London: Collet's, 1962), 63.

30. Santeri Levas, *Jean Sibelius: A Personal Portrait*, trans. Percy M. Young (London: Dent, 1972), 120.

31. Serge Moreux, *Béla Bartók*, trans. G. S. Fraser and Erik de Mauny (London: Harvill Press, 1953), 10.

32. Claude Samuel, *Conversations with Olivier Messiaen*, trans. Felix Aprahamian (London: Stainer & Bell, 1976), 118.

33. Marc Blitzstein, "Towards a New Form," *Musical Quarterly* 20 (1934): 214.

34. Alexander Wheelock Thayer, *Life of Beethoven* (Princeton: Princeton University Press, 1967), 164.

35. Ibid., 273.

36. Karl Geiringer, *Haydn: A Creative Life in Music* (London: Allen & Unwin, 1947), 170.

37. John Warrack, *Carl Maria von Weber* (London: Cambridge University Press, 1968), 98–99.

38. Ibid., 100.

39. Hector Berlioz, *The Life of Hector Berlioz, as Written by Himself in His Letters and Memoirs* (London: Dent, 1912), 60.

40. *Hector Berlioz: A Selection from His Letters*, ed. and trans. Humphrey Searle (New York: Vienna House, 1973), 77.

41. Ibid., 157.

42. Ibid., 188.

43. Ibid., 195.

44. *Richard Wagner's Prose Works*, trans. W. Ashton Ellis (London: Kegan Paul, 1896), 83.

45. Letter from Liszt to Wilhelm von Lenz, 1852, quoted in George R. Marek, *Beethoven: Biography of a Genius* (New York: Funk & Wagnalls, 1969), 638.

46. Richard Heuberger, *Erinnerungen an Johannes Brahms: Tagebuchnotizen aus den Jahren 1875–1897,* ed. K. Hofman (Tutzing, 1970).

47. Modeste Tchaikovsky, *The Life and Letters of Peter Ilich Tchaikovsky*, ed. and trans. Rosa Newmarch (New York: Vienna House, 1973), vol. 2, 517–18.

48. Natalie Bauer-Lechner, *Recollections of Gustav Mahler*, trans. Dika Newlin (London: Faber, 1980), 29–30.

49. Max Graf, *Legend of a Musical City* (New York, 1945), quoted in *The Book of Musical Anecdotes*, ed. Norman Lebrecht (London: Andre Deutsch, 1985), 187.

50. Letter to Egon Petri, 1916, quoted in E. J. Dent, *Ferruccio Busoni* (London: Oxford University Press, 1933), 230.

51. Artur Schnabel, *My Life and Music* (Gerrard's Cross: Colin Smith, 1961), 220–21.

52. Walter Riezler, *Beethoven* (Zurich, 1936), trans. G.D.H. Pidcock (New York: Vienna House, 1972), 9.

53. Hanns Eisler, "Thoughts on the Anniversary of Beethoven's Death" (1952), in *Hanns Eisler: A Rebel in Music*, trans. Marjorie Meyer (Berlin [GDR]: Seven Seas Books, 1978), 168.

54. Ralph Vaughan Williams, "Musical Autobiography," in Hubert Foss, *Ralph Vaughan Williams* (London: Harrap, 1952), 23.

55. Michael Kennedy, *Britten* (London: Dent, 1981), 121.

56. *A Delius Companion*, ed. Christopher Redwood (London: John Calder, 1976), 59.

57. Natalie Bauer-Lechner, *Recollections of Gustav Mahler*, trans. Dika Newlin (London: Faber, 1980), 161.

58. *Cosima Wagner's Diaries*, trans. Geoffrey Skelton, vol. 1 (London: Collins, 1978), 845.

59. Donald Francis Tovey, *Essays in Musical Analysis*, vol. 1, *Symphonies* (London: Oxford University Press, 1935), 27.

60. *Cosima Wagner's Diaries*, trans. Geoffrey Skelton, vol. 1 (London: Collins, 1978), 183.

61. Ibid., 378.

62. Lewis Foreman, *Bax: A Composer and His Times* (London: Scolar Press, 1983), 242.

63. George Grove, *Beethoven and His Nine Symphonies*, 3d ed. (New York: Dover, 1962), 98.

64. Marion M. Scott, *Beethoven* (London: Dent, 1934), 169–70.

65. *Cosima Wagner's Diaries*, trans. Geoffrey Skelton, vol. 1 (London: Collins, 1978), 677.

66. Hector Berlioz, *The Memoirs of Hector Berlioz*, trans. David Cairns (London: Panther, 1970), 122.

67. *Cosima Wagner's Diaries*, trans. Geoffrey Skelton, vol. 1 (London: Collins, 1978), 586.

68. Henry-Louis de La Grange, *Mahler*, vol. 1 (London: Gollancz, 1974), 538.

69. Donald Francis Tovey, *Essays in Musical Analysis*, vol. 1, *Symphonies* (London: Oxford University Press, 1935), 38.

70. Hubert Parry, *The Art of Music* (London, Oxford University Press, 1893), 284.

71. George Grove, *Beethoven and His Nine Symphonies*, 3d ed. (New York: Dover, 1962), 179.

72. Donald Francis Tovey, *Essays in Musical Analysis*, vol. 1, *Symphonies* (London: Oxford University Press, 1935), 47.

73. Hector Berlioz, *A travers chants* (Paris, 1862); English trans. 1913–18, ed. L. Guichard (Paris, 1971), 1: 71.

74. Henry-Louis de La Grange, *Mahler*, vol. 1 (London: Gollancz, 1974), 542.

75. Joan Chissell, *Schumann*, (London: Dent, 1948), 211.

76. George Grove, *Beethoven and His Nine Symphonies*, 3d ed. (New York: Dover, 1962), 244.

77. Ibid., 270.

78. Ibid., 37.

79. Felix Weingartner, "On the Performance of Beethoven's Symphonies," trans. Jessie Crosland in *On Music and Conducting* (New York: Dover, 1969), 163.

80. George Grove, *Beethoven and His Nine Symphonies*, 3d ed. (New York: Dover, 1962), 234.

81. Ibid., 279.

82. Felix Weingartner, "On the Performance of Beethoven's Symphonies," trans. Jessie Crosland, in *On Music and Conducting* (New York: Dover, 1969), 169.

83. *Cosima Wagner's Diaries*, trans. Geoffrey Skelton, vol. 1 (London: Collins, 1978), 600.

84. *The Music Lover's Miscellany*, ed. Eric Blom (London: Gollancz, 1935), 75–76, quoting from Spohr's autobiography.

85. Sergei Bertenssen and Jay Leyda, *Sergei Rachmaninoff: A Lifetime in Music* (London: Allen & Unwin, 1965), 145.

86. Mina Curtiss, *Bizet and His World* (London: Secker & Warburg, 1959), 294.

87. Claude Debussy, *M. Croche antidilettante*, Paris, 1901, English trans. 1927.

88. Ibid.

89. Ernest Newman, *Wagner as Man and Artist* (London: Dent, 1914), 158.

90. *Verdi: The Man in His Letters*, edited and selected by Franz Werfel and Paul Stefan, translated by Edward Downes (New York: Vienna House, 1973), 344.

91. Ralph Vaughan Williams, *National Music and Other Essays*, 2d ed. (London, Oxford University Press, 1987), 83–84.

92. Igor Stravinsky and Robert Craft, *Dialogues and a Diary* (London: Faber, 1968), 122–23.

93. Richard Wagner, *My Life* (London: Constable, 1911) 42.

94. *Correspondence of Wagner and Liszt*, trans. Francis Hueffer, ed W. Ashton Ellis, 2d ed. (New York: Vienna House, 1973), 2: 92.

95. Frederick Goldbeck, *Twentieth-Century Composers*, vol. 4, France, Italy, and Spain (London: Weidenfeld & Nicolson, 1974), 15.

96. Henry-Louis de La Grange, *Mahler*, vol. 1 (London: Gollancz, 1974), 645.

97. *Cosima Wagner's Diaries*, trans. Geoffrey Skelton, vol. 1 (London: Collins, 1978), 805.

98. Richard Wagner, *My Life* (London: Constable, 1911), 30.

99. Edward Lockspeiscr, *Debussy: His Life and Mind*, (Cambridge: Cambridge University Press, 1978), 2:66.

100. Igor Stravinsky and Robert Craft, *Retrospectives and Conclusions* (New York: Knopf, 1969), 142.

101. Ernest Newman, *Wagner as Man and Artist* (London: Dent, 1914), 153.

102. Ronald Taylor, *Richard Wagner, His Life, Art and Thought* (London: Granada, 1983), 56–57.

103. Herbert Weinstock, *Rossini: A Biography* (London: Oxford University Press, 1968), 320.

104. *Verdi: The Man in His Letters*, edited and selected by Franz Werfel and Paul Stefan, translated by Edward Downes (New York: Vienna House, 1973), 431.

105. Arnold Schoenberg, *Style and Idea*, ed. Leonard Stein, trans. Leo Black (London: Faber, 1984), 474.

106. Ibid., 244–45.

107. George Perle, "Berg," in *The New Grove Dictionary of Music and Musicians* (London: Macmillan, 1980), 2: 526.

108. Joan Peyser, *Boulez: Composer, Conductor, Enigma* (London: Cassell, 1977), 50.

109. *Testimony, the Memoirs of Dmitri Shostakovich*, related to and edited by Solomon Volkov (London: Hamish Hamilton, 1979), 30–31.

110. Jaroslav Vogel, *Leoš Janáček*, trans. Geraldine Thomsen-Muchová (Prague: Artia, 1982), 369.

111. Joan Peyser, *Boulez: Composer, Conductor, Enigma* (London: Cassell, 1977), 69–70.

112. Hyman Sandow, *Musical America*, 18 August 1928.

113. *Robert Schumann: The Man and His Music*, ed. Alan Walker (London: Barrie & Jenkins, 1972), 184.

114. Ibid.

115. Richard Wagner, *My Life* (London: Constable, 1911), 234.

116. Ibid.

117. Ibid., 235.

118. Ibid., 628.

119. *Felix Mendelssohn: Letters*, ed. G. Selden-Goth (New York: Vienna House, 1973), 244–45.

120. Ibid., 230.

121. *Verdi: The Man in His Letters*, edited and selected by Franz Werfel and Paul Stefan, translated by Edward Downes (New York: Vienna House, 1973), 363.

122. *Interviews and Encounters with Verdi*, ed. Marcello Conati, trans. Richard Stokes (London: Gollancz, 1984), p. 170.

123. *Correspondence of Wagner and Liszt*, trans. Francis Hueffer, ed. W. Ashton Ellis, 2d ed. (New York: Vienna House, 1973), 2:104.

124. Mina Curtiss, *Bizet and His World* (London: Secker & Warburg, 1959), 20.

125. Edward Lockspeiser, *Debussy: His Life and Mind* (New York: Macmillan, 1962), 1:171.

126. M. D. Calvocoressi, *Musicians Gallery* (London: Faber, 1933), 54.

127. Willi Schuh, *Richard Strauss: A Chronicle of the Early Years*, trans. Mary Whittall, (Cambridge: Cambridge University Press, 1982), 207.

128. Ibid., 206–7.

129. Ibid., 207.

130. Ibid., 208.

131. Igor Stravinsky, *Poetics of Music* (New York: Vintage, 1956), 74.

132. Claude Samuel, *Conversations with Olivier Messiaen*, trans. Felix Aprahamian (London: Stainer & Bell, 1976), 26.

133. Hubert Foss, *Ralph Vaughan Williams* (London, Harrap, 1950), 31.

134. Henry-Louis de La Grange, *Mahler*, vol. 1 (London: Gollancz, 1974), 381–82.

135. Mina Curtiss, *Bizet and His World* (London: Secker & Warburg, 1959), 426–27.

136. Hubert Foss, *Ralph Vaughan Williams* (London: Harrap, 1950), 25.

137. David Brown, *Tchaikovsky: The Crisis Years, 1874–1878* (London: Gollancz, 1982), 59.

138. Paul Horgan, *Encounters with Stravinksy* (London: Bodley Head, 1972), 139.

139. Marc Blitzstein, "Towards a New Form," *Musical Quarterly* 20 (1934): 214.

140. *Verdi: The Man in His Letters,* edited and selected by Franz Werfel and Paul Stefan, translated by Edward Downes (New York: Vienna House, 1973), 337.

141. Nicolai Rimsky-Korsakov, *My Musical Life*, trans. J. A. Joffe (London: Secker & Warburg, 1924), quoted in *The Music Lover's Anthology* (London: Winchester Publications, 1948), 89.

142. David Brown, *Tchaikovsky: The Crisis Years, 1874–1878* (London: Gollancz, 1982), 229.

143. Nicolai Rimsky-Korsakov, *My Musical Life*, trans. J. A. Joffe (London: Secker and Warburg, 1924), quoted in *The Music Lover's Anthology* (London: Winchester Publications, 1948), 87.

144. *Testimony, The Memoirs of Dmitri Shostakovich*, related to and edited by Solomon Volkov (London: Hamish Hamilton, 1979), 122–23.

145. Claude Samuel, *Conversations with Olivier Messiaen*, trans. Felix Aprahamian (London: Stainer & Bell, 1976), 111.

146. Peter Heyworth, *Profiles: Taking Leave of Predecessors - 11, New Yorker*, March 31, 1973, p. 46.

147. Royal S. Brown, *An Interview with Bernard Herrmann (1911–1975) High Fidelity*, September 1976, p. 67.

148. *Robert Schumann: The Man and His Music*, ed. Alan Walker (London: Barrie & Jenkins, 1972), 181–82.

149. Richard Wagner, *My Life* (London, Constable, 1911), 847.

150. *Cosima Wagner's Diaries*, trans. Geoffrey Skelton, vol. 1 (London: Collins, 1978), 778.

151. Ibid., 876.

152. Ernest Newman, *Hugo Wolf* (New York: Dover, 1966), 36.

153. J. Lawrence Erb, *Brahms* (London: Dent, 1925), 131.

154. Modeste Tchaikovsky, *The Life and Letters of Peter Ilich Tchaikovsky*, ed. and trans. Rosa Newmarch (New York: Vienna House, 1973), vol. 1:240–41.

155. *Pleasures of Music*, ed. Jacques Barzun (London, Cassell, 1977), 351.

156. Alma Mahler, *Gustav Mahler: Memories and Letters*, trans. Basil Creighton (London: John Murray, 1946), 181.

157. Natalie Bauer-Lechner, *Recollections of Gustav Mahler*, trans. Dika Newlin (London: Faber, 1980), 142–43.

158. Henry-Louis de La Grange, *Mahler*, vol. 1 (London: Gollancz, 1974), 560–61.

159. *Revue Musicale de la S.I.M.* (Paris), March 1912, quoted in Arbie Orenstein, *Ravel: Man and Musician*, (New York: Columbia University Press, 1975).

160. Michael Kennedy, *Britten* (London: Dent, 1981), 121.

161. Pierre Bernac, *Francis Poulenc: The Man and His Songs* (London: Gollancz, 1977), 34–35.

162. Vera Stravinsky and Robert Craft, *Stravinsky in Pictures and Documents* (London: Hutchinson, 1979), 204.

163. Michael Tippett, obituary in *Listener*, 16 December 1976, 791.

164. *Remembering Britten*, ed. Alan Blyth (London: Hutchinson, 1981), 151.

165. Robert Craft, *Stravinsky: Chronicle of a Friendship, 1948–1971* (New York: Knopf, 1972), 258.

166. George Henschel, *Musings and Memories* (1918), quoted in *The Book of Musical Anecdotes*, ed. Norman Lebrecht (London: Andre Deutsch, 1985), 214.

167. Richard Specht, *Johannes Brahms*, quoted in *The Music Lover's Miscellany*, ed. Eric Blom (London: Gollancz, 1935), 91–92.

168. Felix Weingartner, *Buffets and Rewards*, trans. M. Wolff (London: Hutchinson, 1937), 88.

169. Robert Taylor, *Wagner* (London: Granada, 1979), 402.

170. Ibid., 342.

171. Ernest Newman, *Hugo Wolf* (New York: Dover, 1966), 38.

172. Natalie Bauer-Lechner, *Recollections of Gustav Mahler*, trans. Dika Newlin (London: Faber, 1980), 37.

173. Henry-Louis de La Grange, *Mahler*, vol. 1 (London: Gollancz, 1974), 555.

174. Alma Mahler, *Gustav Mahler: Memories and Letters*, trans. Basil Creighton (London: John Murray, 1946), 89.

175. John Bird, *Percy Grainger* (Melbourne: Macmillan, 1977), 82.

176. Robert Craft, *Stravinsky: Chronicle of a Friendship, 1948–1971* (New York: Knopf, 1972), 69.

177. Aaron Copland, "The New Music," in *The New Music Lover's Handbook*, ed. Elie Siegmeister (New York: Harvey House, 1973), 542–43.

178. Constant Lambert, *Music Ho!* (London: Penguin, 1948), 141.

179. Aaron Copland, "Carlos Chávez—Mexican Composer," originally published in *New Republic*, reprinted in *American Composers on American Music*, ed. Henry Cowell (Stanford University Press, 1933).

180. Alexander Wheelock Thayer, *Life of Beethoven* (Princeton: Princeton University Press, 1967), 683.

181. Ronald Taylor, *Robert Schumann: His Life and Work* (London: Granada, 1982), 105–6.

182. Franz Liszt, *F. Chopin* (Paris, 1852), trans. M. Walker Cooke (London, 1877), 146–48.

183. *Felix Mendelssohn: Letters*, ed. G. Selden-Goth (New York: Vienna House, 1973), 237; Arthur Hedley, *Chopin* (London: Dent, 1947), 51.

184. Mina Curtiss, *Bizet and His World* (London: Secker & Warburg, 1959), 190.

185. Roger Nichols, *Ravel Remembered* (London: Faber, 1987), 110.

186. Claude Samuel, *Conversations with Olivier Messiaen*, trans. Felix Aprahamian (London: Stainer & Bell, 1976), 73.

187. *Prokofiev by Prokofiev*, ed. David H. Appel, trans. Guy Daniels (Garden City, N.Y.: Doubleday, 1979), 228.

188. Igor Stravinsky and Robert Craft, *Retrospectives and Conclusions* (New York: Knopf, 1969), 252.

189. *Mozart's Letters*, ed. Eric Blom, trans. Emily Anderson (London: Pelican, 1956), 210–11.

190. Igor Stravinsky and Robert Craft, *Retrospectives and Conclusions* (New York: Knopf, 1969), 44.

191. Virgil Thomson, *Music Reviewed, 1940–1954* (New York: Vintage, 1967), 231–32.

192. Roger Nichols, *Ravel Remembered* (London: Faber, 1987), 101.

193. Arbie Orenstein, *Ravel: Man and Musician* (New York: Columbia University Press, 1975), 127.

194. Roger Nichols, *Ravel Remembered* (London: Faber, 1987), 67.

195. *Morning Post* (London), 10 July 1922.

196. László Eösze, *Zoltán Kodály: His Life and Work*, trans. István Farkas and Gyula Gulyás (London: Collet's, 1962), 60.

197. Ibid., 60–61.

198. Edward Lockspeiser, *Debussy: His Life and Mind* (Cambridge: Cambridge University Press, 1978), 2:270.

199. *Revue Musicale* 1947, translated by Nicolas Slonimsky, *Lexicon of Musical Invective*, 2d ed. (Seattle: University of Washington Press, 1969), 102.

200. J. Harding, *Saint-Saëns and His Circle* (London: Chapman & Hall, 1965), 215.

201. *Semaine Musicale* (Paris), 11 November 1927, translated by Nicolas Slonimsky, *Lexicon of Musical Invective*, 2d ed. (Seattle: University of Washington Press, 1969), 103.

202. Igor Stravinsky, *Igor Stravinsky: An Autobiography* (New York: Norton, 1962), 18.

203. Igor Stravinsky and Robert Craft, *Retrospectives and Conclusions* (New York: Knopf, 1969), 284.

204. *A Delius Companion*, ed. Christopher Redwood (London: John Calder, 1976), 59.

205. Serge Moreux, *Béla Bartók*, trans. G. S. Fraser and Erik de Mauny (London: Harvill Press, 1953), 92.

206. Claude Samuel, *Conversations with Olivier Messiaen*, trans. Felix Aprahamian (London: Stainer & Bell, 1976), 36.

207. Pierre Boulez, *Relevés d'apprenti* (Paris, 1966), trans. Herbert Weinstock (New York: Knopf, 1968), 35.

208. Aaron Copland, *What to Listen for in Music* (New York: Mentor, 1953), 46.

209. M. D. Calvocoressi, *Musicians Gallery* (London: Faber, 1933), 114.

210. Constant Lambert, *Music Ho!* (London: Penguin, 1948), 19.

211. Ibid., 21.

212. Harriet Cohen, *A Bundle of Time* (London: 1969), quoted in *The Book of Musical Anecdotes*, ed. Norman Lebrecht (London: Andre Deutsch, 1985), 261.

213. Ernest Bloch, "Man and Music," *Seven Arts*, March 1917, reprinted in *Musical Quarterly* 19 (1933): 379.

214. Christopher Palmer, *Delius* (London: Duckworth, 1976), 189.

215. Ibid., ix.

216. Ibid., 150–51.

217. Constant Lambert, *Music Ho!* (London: Penguin, 1948), 188.

218. *A Delius Companion*, ed. Christopher Redwood (London: John Calder, 1976), 119.

219. John Bird, *Percy Grainger* (Melbourne: Macmillan, 1977), 204.

220. J. Ma Corredor, *Conversations with Casals*, trans. André Mangeot (New York: Dutton, 1956), 66–67.

221. Egon Gartenberg, *Vienna: Its Musical Heritage* (Philadelphia: Pennsylvania State University Press, 1968), 124.

222. Alec Robertson, *Dvořák* (London: Dent, 1945), 75.

223. Ibid., 114.

224. Michael Kennedy, *Portrait of Elgar* (London: Oxford University Press, 1968), 101.

225. British Broadcasting Corporation broadcast in 1957, "The Fifteenth Variation."

226. Interview in *Guardian* (London), 29 February 1972.

227. Eric Fenby, *Delius as I Knew Him* (London: Icon, 1966), 124.

228. *A Delius Companion*, ed. Christopher Redwood (London: John Calder, 1976), 60.

229. Michael Kennedy, *Richard Strauss* (London: Dent, 1976), 37.

230. Virgil Thomson, *Music Reviewed 1940–1954* (New York: Vintage, 1967), 4.

231. Vincent d'Indy, *César Franck*, trans. Rosa Newmarch (New York: Dover, 1965), 172–73.

232. Ibid., 89.

233. H. H. Stuckenschmidt, *Maurice Ravel: Variations on His Life and Work*, trans. Samuel R. Rosenbaum (Philadelphia: Chilton Book Company, 1968), 138–39.

234. J. Hardy, *Saint-Saëns and His Circle* (London: Chapman Hall, 1965), 219.

235. *A Delius Companion*, ed. Christopher Redwood (London: John Calder, 1976), 60.

236. Leonard Bernstein, "A Nice Gershwin Tune," *Atlantic Monthly,* April 1955, 40–41.

237. Ibid.

238. *The Book of Musical Anecdotes*, ed. Norman Lebrecht (London: Andre Deutsch, 1985), 296.

239. *Testimony, the Memoirs of Dmitri Shostakovich*, related to and edited by Solomon Volkov (London: Hamish Hamilton, 1979), 124.

240. Igor Stravinsky and Robert Craft, *Retrospectives and Conclusions* (New York: Knopf, 1969), 201.

241. M. D. Calvocoressi, *Musicians Gallery* (London: Faber, 1933), 54.

242. James Bakst, *A History of Russian - Soviet Music* (New York: Dodd, Mead, 1962), 201.

243. Ibid., 67.

244. Ibid., quoting Berlioz in *Journal des débats*, 16 April 1845.

245. Alfred Einstein, *Gluck*, trans. Eric Blom (London: Dent, 1936), 179.

246. Hector Berlioz, *The Memoirs of Hector Berlioz*, trans. David Cairns (London: Panther, 1970), 91.

247. *Verdi: The Man in His Letters*, edited and selected by Franz Werfel and Paul Stefan, translated by Edward Downes (New York: Vienna House, 1973), 431.

248. Richard Wagner, *My Life* (London: Constable, 1911), 408.

249. Henry-Louis de La Grange, *Mahler*, vol. 1 (London: Gollancz, 1974), 500–501.

250. *Interviews and Encounters with Verdi*, ed. Marcello Conati, trans. Richard Stokes (London: Gollancz, 1984), 170.

251. *Verdi: The Man in His Letters,* edited and selected by Franz Werfel and Paul Stefan, translated by Edward Downes (New York: Vienna House, 1973), 346.

252. Mina Curtiss, *Bizet and His World* (London: Secker & Warburg, 1959), 84.

253. M. D. Calvocoressi, *Musicians Gallery* (London: Faber, 1933), 53.

254. Vladimir Jankelevitch, *Ravel*, trans. Margaret Crosland (London: John Calder, 1959), 163.

255. *A Delius Companion*, ed. Christopher Redwood (London: John Calder, 1976), 59.

256. *The Musical Companion*, ed. A. L. Bacharach (London: Gollancz, 1934), 262.

257. Edwin Evans, *Tchaikovsky*, rev. ed. (London: Dent, 1935), 47–48.

258. Karl Geiringer, *Haydn: A Creative Life in Music* (London: Allen & Unwin, 1947), 103.

259. J. Cuthbert Hadden, *Haydn* (London: Dent, 1934), 83.

260. Alexander Wheelock Thayer, *Life of Beethoven* (Princeton: Princeton University Press, 1967), 920.

261. Ibid., 871.

262. Ibid., 1024.

263. Richard Wagner, *My Life* (London: Constable, 1911), 634–35.

264. *Felix Mendelssohn: Letters*, ed. G. Selden-Goth (New York: Vienna House, 1973), 257.

265. Arnold Schoenberg, *Style and Idea*, ed. Leonard Stein, trans. Leo Black (London: Faber, 1984), 117–18.

266. Igor Stravinsky and Robert Craft, *Retrospectives and Conclusions* (New York: Knopf, 1969), 287.

267. Aaron Copland, *The New Music 1900–1960* (New York: Norton, 1941), 163–64.

268. Virgil Thomson, *Music Reviewed, 1940–1954* (New York: Vintage, 1967), 16.

269. Ibid., 359.

270. *Mozart: The Man and the Artist Revealed in His Own Words,* comp. Friederich Kerst, trans. Henry Edward Krehbiel (New York: Dover, 1965), 42.

271. *The Letters of Mozart and His Family*, ed. and trans. Emily Anderson, 3d ed. (London: Macmillan, 1985), 892.

272. Karl Geiringer, *Haydn: A Creative Life in Music* (London: Allen & Unwin, 1947), 170.

273. Egon Gartenberg, *Mahler: the Man and His Music* (New York: Schirmer, 1979), 193.

274. Ernest Newman, *Richard Strauss* (London: John Lane, Bodley Head, 1908), xii.

275. Robert Chesterman, *Conversations with Conductors* (London: Robson, 1976), 83.

276. *The Book of Musical Anecdotes,* ed. Norman Lebrecht (London: Andre Deutsch, 1985), 289.

277. Interview in *Guardian* (London), 30 July 1976.

278. Peter Heyworth, *Profiles: Taking Leave of Predecessors-II, New Yorker,* March 31, 1973, p. 56.

279. Geoffrey Skelton, *Paul Hindemith: The Man behind the Music* (London: Gollancz, 1975), 75.

280. Michael Kennedy, *Richard Strauss* (London: Dent, 1976), 72.

281. Santeri Levas, *Jean Sibelius: A Personal Portrait,* trans. Percy M. Young (London: Dent, 1972), 73.

282. Constant Lambert, *Music Ho!* (London: Penguin, 1948), 184.

283. Virgil Thomson, *Music Reviewed, 1940–1954* (New York: Vintage, 1967), 35.

284. Quoted by Vernon Duke, "Gershwin, Schillinger and Dukelshy," *Musical Quarterly* 33 (January 1947): 108.

285. Aaron Copland, *What to Listen for in Music* (New York: Mentor, 1953), 121.

286. Henry Cowell and Sidney Cowell, *Charles Ives and His Music* (New York, 1955) quoted in *The Book of Musical Anecdotes,* ed. Norman Lebrecht (London: Andre Deutsch, 1985), 289.

287. Igor Stravinsky and Robert Craft, *Retrospectives and Conclusions* (New York: Knopf, 1969), 30.

288. Bernard Herrmann, *Trend* (New York), September–November 1932, 99–101.

289. Boris Schwarz, "Khachaturian," in *The New Grove Dictionary of Music and Musicians,* (London: Macmillan, 1980), 10:48.

290. *Bela Bartók Essays,* ed. Benjamin Suchoff (London: Faber, 1976), 469.

291. David Brown, *Tchaikovsky: The Crisis Years, 1874–1878,* (London: Gollancz, 1982), 260.

292. Vincent d'Indy, *César Franck,* trans. Rosa Newmarch (New York: Dover, 1965), 172.

293. Alma Mahler, *Gustav Mahler: Memories and Letters,* trans. Basil Creighton (London: John Murray, 1946), 99.

294. Sergei Bertenssen and Jay Leyda, *Sergei Rachmaninoff: A Lifetime in Music* (London: Allen & Unwin, 1965), 137.

295. Eleanor Perényi, *Liszt* (London: Weidenfeld and Nicolson, 1974), 58.

296. B. Litzmann, *Clara Schumann: An Artist's Life* (Leipzig, 1902) trans. W. H. Hadow (London: Macmillan, 1913), 285.

297. Joan Chissell, *Schumann* (London: Dent, 1948), 209.

298. *Correspondence of Wagner and Liszt,* trans. Francis Hueffer, ed. W. Ashton Ellis, 2d ed. (New York: Vienna House, 1973), 2:159.

299. Wilfrid Blunt, *On Wings of Song: A Biography of Felix Mendelssohn* (New York: Scribner's, 1974), 148.

300. Harold Schonberg, *The Great Pianists* (New York: Simon & Schuster, 1963), 141.

301. Modeste Tchaikovsky, *The Life and Letters of Peter Ilich Tchaikovsky,* ed. and trans. Rosa Newmarch (New York: Vienna House, 1973), vol. 2, 412.

302. Willi Schuh, *Richard Strauss: A Chronicle of the Early Years,* trans. Mary Whittall (Cambridge: Cambridge University Press, 1982), 210.

303. Ibid., 208.

304. Ibid., 209.

305. Natalie Bauer-Lechner, *Recollections of Gustav Mahler*, trans. Dika Newlin (London: Faber, 1980), 30.

306. *Bela Bartók Essays*, ed. Benjamin Suchoff (London: Faber, 1976), 505.

307. Ibid., 502.

308. Ibid., 452.

309. M. D. Calvocoressi, *Musicians Gallery* (London: Faber, 1933), 54.

310. Igor Stravinsky and Robert Craft, *Retrospectives and Conclusions* (New York: Knopf, 1969), 204.

311. Alma Mahler, *Gustav Mahler: Memories and Letters*, trans. Basil Creighton (London: John Murray, 1946), 190–91.

312. Arnold Schoenberg, *Style and Idea*, ed. Leonard Stein, trans. Leo Black (London: Faber, 1984), 447.

313. *Rivalry and Friendship: Gustav Mahler-Richard Strauss Correspondence, 1888–1911*, ed. Herta Blaukopf, trans. Edmund Jephcott (London: Faber, 1984), 75.

314. *A Working Friendship: The Correspondence between Richard Strauss and Hugo von Hofmannsthal*, trans. Hanns Hammelmann and Ewald Osers (New York: Vienna House, 1974), 495.

315. Ralph Vaughan Williams, *National Music and Other Essays*, 2d ed. (London: Oxford University Press, 1987), 187.

316. Robert Chesterman, *Conversations with Conductors* (London: Robson, 1976), 108.

317. *Gustav Mahler in Vienna*, ed. Sigrid Wiesmann (London: Thames & Hudson, 1977), 17.

318. Aaron Copland, *The New Music, 1900–1960* (New York: Norton, 1969), 33.

319. Helena Matheopoulos, *Maestro: Encounters with Conductors of Today* (London: Hutchinson, 1982), 15.

320. Leonard Bernstein: "Mahler: His Time Has Come," *High Fidelity*, April 1967, reprinted in *Findings* (New York: Simon & Schuster, 1982) 255.

321. Ibid., 255.

322. Willi Reich, *Alban Berg*, trans. Cornelius Cardew (New York: Vienna House, 1974), 71.

323. *Interviews and Encounters with Verdi*, ed. Marcello Conati, trans. Richard Stokes (London: Gollancz, 1984), 221.

324. Edward Lockspeiser, *Debussy: His Life and Mind* (New York: Macmillan, 1962), 1:170.

325. *Hector Berlioz: A Selection from his Letters*, ed. and trans. Humphrey Searle (New York: Vienna House, 1973), 43.

326. Ibid., 37.

327. Ibid, 101.

328. Joan Chissell, *Schumann* (London: Dent, 1948), 66–67.

329. *Robert Schumann: The Man and His Music*, ed. Alan Walker (London: Barrie & Jenkins, 1972), 196.

330. Ronald Taylor, *Robert Schumann: His Life and Work* (London: Granada, 1982), 265.

331. Ernest Newman, *A Study of Wagner* (New York: Vienna House, 1974), 270.

332. Ibid., 153.

333. Santeri Levas, *Jean Sibelius: A Personal Portrait,* trans. Percy M. Young (London: Dent, 1972), 68. ˅

334. Interview with Alan Blyth, *Gramophone,* November 1967, 252.

335. Joan Peyser, *Boulez: Composer, Conductor, Enigma* (London: Cassell, 1977), 31.

336. Igor Stravinsky and Robert Craft, *Retrospectives and Conclusions* (New York: Knopf, 1969), 65.

337. Ibid., 18.

338. Ibid., 65.

339. Witold Lutosławski, "Where the Future of Music Is Concerned, I'm an Optimist," *Finnish Music Quarterly* (Helsinki), 1988, no. 2:47.

340. Aaron Copland, *What to Listen for in Music* (New York: Mentor, 1953), 125.

341. Igor Stravinsky and Robert Craft, *Retrospectives and Conclusions* (New York: Knopf, 1969), 58.

342. *The Letters of Mozart and His Family,* ed. Emily Anderson, 3d ed. (London: Macmillan, 1985), 886.

343. H. E. Jacob, *Joseph Haydn: His Art, Times, and Glory* (London: Gollancz, 1950), 145.

344. Alexander Wheelock Thayer, *Life of Beethoven* (Princeton: Princeton University Press, 1967), 366.

345. Ibid., 209.

346. Ibid., 776.

347. Martin Cooper, *Beethoven: The Last Decade, 1817–1827* (London: Oxford University Press, 1970), 127.

348. "Sayings of Beethoven" *Musical Quarterly* 13 (1927): 202.

349. Ibid.

350. *Allgemeine Musikalische Zeitung,* 6 June 1832, trans. Ernest Newman, in *The Music Lover's Miscellany,* ed. Eric Blom, (London: Gollancz, 1935), 72–73.

351. *Franz Schubert's Letters and Other Writings,* ed. Otto Deutsch, trans. Venetia Savile (New York: Vienna House, 1974), 25–26.

352. Hector Berlioz, *The Memoirs of Hector Berlioz,* trans. David Cairns (London: Panther, 1970), 108.

353. Herbert Weinstock, *Rossini: A Biography* (London: Oxford University Press, 1968), 309.

354. Ibid., 320.

355. Igor Stravinsky, *Poetics of Music* (New York: Vintage, 1956), 76.

356. Peter Latham, *Brahms* (London: Dent, 1948), 74.

357. *Cosima Wagner's Diaries,* trans. Geoffrey Skelton, vol. 1 (London: Collins, 1978), 579.

358. Modeste Tchaikovsky, *The Life and Letters of Peter Ilich Tchaikovsky,* ed. and trans. Rosa Newmarch (New York: Vienna House, 1973), vol. 2, 518.

359. Mina Curtiss, *Bizet and His World* (London: Secker & Warburg, 1959), 96.

360. Arbie Orenstein, *Ravel: Man and Musician* (New York: Columbia University Press, 1975), 123.

361. Ibid.

362. Roger Nicholas, *Ravel Remembered* (London: Faber, 1987), 110.

363. Artur Schnabel, *My Life and Music* (Gerard's Cross: Colin Smyth, 1970), 122.

364. Santeri Levas, *Jean Sibelius: A Personal Portrait*, trans. Percy M. Young (London: Dent, 1972), 60.

365. Leonard Bernstein, *The Unanswered Question* (Cambridge, Mass.: Harvard University Press, 1976), 49.

366. *High Fidelity*, June 1956.

367. Michael Kennedy, *Britten* (London: Dent, 1981), 101.

368. Claude Samuel, *Conversations with Olivier Messiaen*, trans. Felix Aprahamian (London: Stainer & Bell, 1976), 35.

369. Ibid., 36.

370. Quoted by Percy Grainger, "The Personality of Frederick Delius: Remarkable Article on Dead Composer," *Australian Musical News*, July 1934, 14.

371. *Testimony, the Memoirs of Dmitri Shostakovich*, related and edited by Solomon Volkov (London: Hamish Hamilton, 1979), 46.

372. Herbert Weinstock, *Rossini: A Biography* (London: Oxford University Press, 1968), 309.

373. Martin Cooper, "Mussorgsky," in *The New Grove Dictionary of Music and Musicians* (London: Macmillan, 1980) 12:870.

374. Gerald Abraham, *Rimsky-Korsakov* (London: Duckworth, 1945), 72.

375. César Cui, *St. Petersburg Vedomosti*, 18 February 1874, quoted in Nicolas Slonimsky, *Lexicon of Musical Invective*, 2d ed. (Seattle: University of Washington Press, 1969), 127.

376. *Testimony, the Memoirs of Dmitri Shostakovich*, related to and edited by Solomon Volkov (London: Hamish Hamilton, 1979), 175.

377. Draft of a statement about Mussorgsky, 4 September 1957, illustrated in Vera Stravinksy and Robert Craft, *Stravinsky in Pictures and Documents* (London: Hutchinson, 1979), 439.

378. Letter by Tchaikosvky to his brother Modeste, 29 October 1874, quoted in Nicolas Slonimsky, *Lexicon of Musical Invective*, 2d ed. (Seattle: University of Washington Press, 1969), 127.

379. Modeste Tchaikovsky, *The Life and Letters of Peter Ilich Tchaikovsky* ed. and trans. Rosa Newmarch (New York: Vienna House, 1973), vol. 2, 461.

380. David Brown, *Tchaikovsky: A Biographical and Critical Study*, vol. 2, (London: Victor Gollancz Ltd, 1982), 229.

381. In a review in *Revue Blanche*, quoted by Edward Lockspeiser, "Mussorgsky and Debussy," *Musical Quarterly* 23 (1937): 426.

382. Frederick Goldbeck, *Twentieth-Century Composers*, vol. 4, *France, Italy, and Spain* (London: Weidenfeld & Nicolson, 1974), 16.

383. Leonard Bernstein, *Findings* (New York: Simon & Schuster, 1982), 242–43.

384. Hans Gal, *Richard Wagner,* trans. Hans-Hubert Schönzeler (New York: Stein & Day, 1976), 116–17.

385. Henry-Louis de La Grange, *Mahler,* vol. 1 (London: Gollancz, 1974), 665.

386. *Interviews and Encounters with Verdi,* ed. Marcello Conati, trans. Richard Stokes (London: Gollancz, 1984), 366.

387. Ibid., 285.

388. *Verdi: The Man in His Letters,* edited and selected by Franz Werfel and Paul Stepan, translated by Edward Downes (New York: Vienna House, 1973), 402.

389. Ibid., 430.

390. James Harding, *Gounod* (London: Allen & Unwin, 1973), 125.

391. Edward Lockspeiser, *Debussy: His Life and Mind,* (New York: Macmillan, 1962), 1:171–72.

392. James Harding, *Erik Satie* (London: Secker & Warburg, 1975), 97.

393. *S. Prokofiev: Autobiography Articles Reminiscences* (Moscow: Foreign Languages Publishing House, 1965), 192.

394. *Testimony, the Memoirs of Dmitri Shostakovich,* related to and edited by Solomon Volkov (London: Hamish Hamilton, 1979), 27.

395. Igor Stravinsky, *Memories and Commentaries* (London: Faber, 1960), 67–68.

396. Aaron Copland, *What to Listen for in Music* (New York: Mentor, 1953), 38.

397. *S. Prokofiev: Autobiography Articles Reminiscences* (Moscow: Foreign Languages Publishing House, 1965), 195.

398. Claude Samuel, *Prokofiev,* trans. Miriam John (New York: Grossman Publishers, 1971), 117.

399. Ibid., 61.

400. Ibid., 108.

401. Interview with Rémy Stricker, *France Culture,* quoted in Marcel Marnat, *Maurice Ravel* (Paris, 1986), again quoted in Roger Nichols, *Ravel Remembered* (London, Faber, 1987), 110.

402. Alma Mahler, *Gustav Mahler: Memories and Letters,* trans. Basil Creighton (London: John Murray, 1946), 178.

403. *Verdi: The Man in His Letters,* edited and selected by Franz Werfel and Paul Stefan, translated by Edward Downes (New York: Vienna House, 1973), 372–73.

404. Igor Stravinsky and Robert Craft, *Retrospectives and Conclusions* (New York: Knopf, 1969), 17–18.

405. "Verdi—A Symposium," *Opera* (London), February 1951, 114–15.

406. Geoffrey Norris, *Rakhmaninov* (London: Dent, 1976), 25.

407. Sergei Bertenssen and Jay Leyda, *Sergei Rachmaninoff: A Lifetime in Music* (London: Allen & Unwin, 1965), 298.

408. *S. Prokofiev: Autobiography Articles Reminiscences* (Moscow: Foreign Languages Publishing House, 1965), 107–8.

409. Alfredo Casella, *Musica d'oggi,* March 1938, quoted in "Music in the Foreign Press—Ravel," *Musical Times* (London), June 1938, 425.

410. László Eösze, *Zoltán Kodály: His Life and Work,* trans. István Farkas and Gyula Gulyás (London: Collet's, 1962), 62.

411. Victor Serov, *Sergei Prokofiev: A Soviet Tragedy* (London: Leslie Frewin, 1968), 100.

412. Ibid., 151.

413. Igor Stravinsky and Robert Craft, *Conversations with Igor Stravinsky* (London: Faber and Faber, 1959), 62.

414. Igor Stravinsky, *Igor Stravinsky: An Autobiography* (New York: Norton, 1962), 37.

415. Manuel de Falla, *On Music and Musicians*, trans. David Urman and J. M. Thomson (London: Boyars, 1979), 93.

416. Rollo Meyers, *Ravel* (London: Duckworth, 1960), 79.

417. Constant Lambert, *Music Ho!* (London: Penguin, 1948), 143.

418. Arthur Honegger, *Incantation aux fossiles* (Lausanne: Editions d'Ouchy, 1948), 91–92.

419. H. H. Stuckenschmidt, *Maurice Ravel: Variations on His Life and Work*, trans. Samuel R. Rosenbaum (Philadelphia: Chilton Book Company, 1968), 235.

420. Hubert Foss, *Ralph Vaughan Williams* (London: Harrap, 1950), 35.

421. Alfred Swan and Katherine Swan, "Reminiscences of Rachmaninov," *Musical Quarterly* 30 (1944): 177–78.

422. Ibid., 178.

423. Sergei Bertenssen and Jay Leyda, *Sergei Rachmaninoff: A Lifetime in Music* (London: Allen & Unwin, 1956), 139.

424. Vera Stravinsky and Robert Craft, *Stravinsky in Pictures and Documents* (London: Hutchinson, 1979), 48.

425. Ibid.

426. Igor Stravinsky, *Igor Stravinsky: An Autobiography* (New York: Norton, 1962), 16.

427. W. J. Turner, *Beethoven: The Search for Reality* (London: Dent, 1927), 187.

428. Alexander Wheelock Thayer, *Life of Beethoven* (Princeton: Princeton University Press, 1967), 955–56.

429. Hector Berlioz, *The Memoirs of Hector Berlioz*, trans. David Cairns (London: Panther, 1970), 90.

430. William Ashbrook, *Donizetti* (London: Cassell, 1965), 274.

431. *Interviews and Encounters with Verdi*, ed. Marcello Conati, trans. Richard Stokes (London: Gollancz, 1984), 170.

432. *Felix Mendelssohn: Letters*, ed. G. Selden-Goth (New York: Vienna House, 1973), 260.

433. Herbert Weinstock, *Rossini: A Biography* (London: Oxford University Press, 1968), 297.

434. Richard Osborne, *Rossini* (London: Dent, 1986), 255.

435. *Shostakovich: The Man and His Music*, ed. Christopher Norris (London: Lawrence & Wishart, 1982), 152.

436. Louis Engel, *Mozart*, quoted in *The Book of Musical Anecdotes*, ed. Norman Lebrecht (London: Andre Deutsch, 1985), 107.

437. J. Harding, *Saint-Saëns* (London: Chapman & Hall, 1965), 209.

438. Ibid., 213.

439. H. H. Stuckenschmidt, *Maurice Ravel: Variations on His Life and Work*,

trans. Samuel R. Rosenbaum (Philadelphia: Chilton Book Company, 1968), 168–69.

440. Vincent d'Indy, *César Franck*, trans. Rosa Newmarch (New York: Dover, 1965), 172.

441. J. Harding, *Saint-Saëns and his Circle* (London: Chapman & Hall, 1965), 209.

442. Igor Stravinsky, *Igor Stravinsky: An Autobiography* (New York: Norton, 1962), 38.

443. Interview with Darius Milhaud, broadcast by the British Broadcasting Corporation, 24 October 1957.

444. Edward Lockspeiser, *Debussy* (London: Dent, 1951,) 48–49.

445. Constant Lambert, *Music Ho!* (London: Penguin, 1948), 93.

446. G. Francesco Malipiero, "Domenico Scarlatti," *Musical Quarterly* 13 (1927): 478.

447. Alma Mahler, *Gustav Mahler: Memories and Letters*, trans. Basil Creighton (London: John Murray, 1946), 92.

448. Arnold Schoenberg, *Style and Idea,* ed. Leonard Stein, trans. Leo Black, (London: Faber, 1984), 42.

449. Maurice Ravel, *Contemporary Music*, Rice Institute pamphlet, April 1928.

450. Santeri Levas, *Jean Sibelius: A Personal Portrait*, trans. Percy M. Young (London: Dent, 1972), 74.

451. Ibid.

452. *A Delius Companion*, ed. Christopher Redwood (London: John Calder, 1976), 61.

453. Cecil Gray, *Musical Chairs* (London: Home & Van Thal, 1948), 198.

454. Ibid., 198–99.

455. In *Noche*, 12 March 1936.

456. Igor Stravinsky and Robert Craft, *Dialogues and a Diary* (Garden City, N.Y.: Doubleday, 1963).

457. Alma Mahler, *And the Bridge Is Love* (London: Hutchinson, 1959), 148.

458. Claude Samuel, *Conversations with Olivier Messiaen*, trans. Felix Aprahamian (London: Stainer & Bell, 1976), 116, 111.

459. Joan Peyser, *Boulez: Composer, Conductor, Enigma* (Cassell: London, 1977), 75.

460. Egon Wellesz, *Arnold Schoenberg* (London: Galliard, 1971), 149.

461. Hanns Eisler, "On Schoenberg" (1935), in *Hanns Eisler: A Rebel in Music*, trans. Marjorie Meyer (Berlin [GDR]: Seven Seas Books, 1978), 75.

462. Charles Rosen, *Schoenberg* (London: Fontana, 1976), 7.

463. Newman Flower, *Franz Schubert: The Man and His Circle* (London: Cassell, 1949), 147.

464. *Robert Schumann: The Man and His Music,* ed. Alan Walker (London: Barrie & Jenkins, 1972), 279.

465. Alfred Einstein, *Schubert*, trans. David Ascoli (London: Cassell, 1951), 335.

466. Ibid., 316–17.

467. *Felix Mendelssohn: Letters*, ed. G. Selden-Goth (New York: Vienna House, 1973), 281.

468. Natalie Bauer-Lechner, *Recollections of Gustav Mahler,* trans. Dika Newlin (London: Faber, 1980), 147.

469. Benjamin Britten, *On Receiving the First Aspen Award* (London: Faber, 1964), 18.

470. Natalie Bauer-Lechner, *Recollections of Gustav Mahler,* trans. Dika Newlin (London: Faber, 1980), 169.

471. Ronald Taylor, *Robert Schumann: His Life and Work* (London: Granada, 1982), 192.

472. Santeri Levas, *Jean Sibelius: A Personal Portrait*, trans. Percy M. Young (London: Dent, 1972), 67.

473. Joan Peyser, *Boulez: Composer, Conductor, Enigma* (London: Cassell, 1977), 209.

474. Igor Stravinsky and Robert Craft, *Retrospectives and Conclusions* (New York: Knopf, 1969), 75.

475. Eric Fenby, *Delius as I Knew Him* (London: Icon, 1966), 195.

476. Victor Seroff, *Sergei Prokofiev: A Soviet Tragedy* (London: Leslie Frewin, 1968), 90.

477. M. D. Calvocoressi and Gerald Abraham, *Masters of Russian Music* (New York: Tudor Publishing Company, 1944), 467.

478. Ibid., 486.

479. Ibid., 467.

480. *Prokofiev by Prokofiev: A Composer's Memoir*, ed. David H. Appel, trans. Guy Daniels (Garden City, N.Y.: Doubleday, 1979), 293.

481. Nicolas Slonimsky, *Lexicon of Musical Invective,* 2d ed. (Seattle: University of Washington Press, 1969), 172.

482. *Shostakovich: The Man and His Music*, ed. Christopher Norris (London: Lawrence & Wishart, 1982), 167.

483. Vera Stravinsky and Robert Craft, *Stravinsky in Pictures and Documents* (London: Hutchinson, 1979), 605.

484. Boris Schwarz, "Shostakovich," in *The New Grove Dictionary of Music and Musicians* (London: Macmillan, 1980), 17: 267.

485. Ibid.

486. Vera Stravinsky and Robert Craft, *Stravinsky in Pictures and Documents* (London: Hutchinson, 1979), 201.

487. Ibid., 201–2.

488. Michael Kennedy, *Britten* (London: Dent, 1981), 23.

489. Constant Lambert, *Music Ho!* (London: Penguin, 1948), 226.

490. Virgil Thomson, *Music Reviewed, 1940–1954* (New York: Vintage, 1967), 4.

491. Erik Tawaststjerna, *Sibelius,* trans. Robert Layton, vol. 1 (London: Faber, 1976), 241.

492. Arbie Orenstein, *Ravel: Man and Musician* (New York: Columbia University Press, 1975), 125.

493. Robert Craft, *Stravinsky: Chronicle of a Friendship, 1948–1971* (New York: Knopf, 1972), 113.

494. David Wooldridge, *Charles Ives: A Portrait* (London: Faber, 1975), 259.

495. Ferdinand Scherchen, introduction to Karl Goldmark, *Notes from the Life of a Viennese Composer* (New York: 1927).

496. J. Lawrence Erb, *Brahms* (London: Dent, 1925), 103.

497. Willi Schuh, *Richard Strauss: A Chronicle of the Early Years,* trans. Mary Whittall (Cambridge: Cambridge University Press, 1982), 207.

498. Natalie Bauer-Lechner, *Recollections of Gustav Mahler,* trans. Dika Newlin (London: Faber, 1980), 128.

499. Ibid., 128.

500. Modeste Tchaikovsky, *The Life and Letters of Peter Tchaikovsky,* ed. and trans. Rosa Newmarch (New York: Vienna House, 1973), vol. 2, 545.

501. Alma Mahler, *Gustav Mahler: Memories and Letters,* trans. Basil Creighton (London: John Murray, 1946), 202.

502. Ibid., 103.

503. Jerrold Northrop Moore, *Edward Elgar* (London: Oxford University Press, 1984), 511.

504. Hélène Jourdan-Morhange, *Ravel et Nous* (Geneva: 1945), 81.

505. Ibid.

506. Aaron Copland, *What to Listen for in Music* (New York: Mentor, 1953), 120.

507. Edward Lockspeiser, *Debussy: His Life and Mind* (Cambridge: Cambridge University Press, 1978), 2:69.

508. Ibid.

509. Ibid.

510. *Béla Bartók Essays,* ed. Benjamin Suchoff (London: Faber, 1976), 445.

511. Ibid., 505.

512. Ibid., 446.

513. Vera Stravinsky and Robert Craft, *Stravinsky in Pictures and Documents* (London: Hutchinson, 1979), 29.

514. Sergei Bertenssen and Jay Leyda, *Sergei Rachmaninoff: A Lifetime in Music* (London: Allen and Unwin, 1965), 130.

515. *Rivalry and Friendship: Gustav Mahler–Richard Strauss Correspondence, 1888–1911,* ed. Herta Blaukopf, trans. Edmund Jephcott (London: Faber, 1984), 85.

516. Michael Kennedy, *Richard Strauss* (London: Dent, 1976), 114–15.

517. Leonard Bernstein, *Findings* (New York: Simon & Schuster, 1982), 299.

518. Frederick Goldbeck, *Twentieth-Century Composers,* vol. 4, *France, Italy, and Spain* (London: Weidenfeld and Nicolson, 1974), 36.

519. Artur Schnabel, *My Life and Music* (Gerrard's Cross: Colin Smyth, 1970), 94.

520. Richard Buckle, *Diaghilev* (London: Weidenfeld and Nicolson, 1979), quoted in *The Book of Musical Anecdotes,* ed. Norman Lebrecht (London: Andre Deutsch, 1985), 305.

521. *Testimony, the Memoirs of Dmitri Shostakovich,* related to and edited by Solomon Volkov (London: Hamish Hamilton, 1979), 24.

522. Ibid.

523. Hanns Eisler, "Basic Questions of Modern Music" (1948), in *Hanns Eisler: A Rebel in Music,* trans. Marjorie Meyer (Berlin [GDR]: Seven Seas Books, 1978), 164.

524. *Tempo,* Winter 1949–50, quoted in *The New Music Lover's Handbook,* ed. Elie Siegmeister (New York: Harvey House, 1973), 34.

525. Marc Blitzstein, "The Phenomenon of Stravinsky," *Musical Quarterly* 21 (1935): 330.

526. Claude Samuel, *Conversations with Olivier Messiaen*, trans. Felix Aprahamian (London: Stainer & Bell, 1976), 117.

527. Constant Lambert, *Music Ho!* (London: Penguin, 1948), 13.

528. Edward Lockspeiser, *Debussy: His Life and Mind* (Cambridge: Cambridge University Press, 1978), 2:182.

529. Ibid., 2:180–81.

530. Victor Seroff, *Sergei Prokofiev: A Soviet Tragedy* (London: Leslie Frewin, 1968), 99.

531. Ibid., 101.

532. *A Delius Companion*, ed. Christopher Redwood (London: John Calder, 1976), 61.

533. Rollo H. Meyers, *Ravel* (London: Duckworth, 1960), 213.

534. Arnold Schoenberg, *Style and Idea*, ed. Leonard Stein, trans. Leo Black (London: Faber, 1975), 482–83.

535. Ibid., 483.

536. Vera Stravinsky and Robert Craft, *Stravinsky in Pictures and Documents* (London: Hutchinson, 1979), 269.

537. Lillian Libman, *And Music at the Close: Stravinsky's Last Years* (London: Macmillan, 1972), 173.

538. Geoffrey Norris, *Rakhmaninov* (London: Dent, 1976), 51–52.

539. Igor Stravinsky, *Poetics of Music* (New York: Vintage, 1956), 83.

540. Vera Stravinsky and Robert Craft, *Stravinsky in Pictures and Documents* (London: Hutchinson, 1979), 201.

541. Letter to *The Times* (London), 17 October 1921.

542. David Brown, *Tchaikovsky: The Crisis Years, 1874–1878* (London: Gollancz, 1982), 218.

543. Ibid.

544. Ibid., 161–62.

545. Natalie Bauer-Lechner, *Recollections of Gustav Mahler*, trans. Dika Newlin (London: Faber, 1980), 166.

546. *Interviews and Encounters with Verdi*, ed. Marcello Conati, trans. Richard Stokes (London: Gollancz, 1984), 20.

547. Herbert Weinstock, *Rossini: A Biography* (London: Oxford University Press, 1968), 284.

548. J. Lawrence Erb, *Brahms* (London: Dent, 1925), 117.

549. Mina Curtiss, *Bizet and His World* (London: Secker & Warburg, 1959), 82.

550. Ibid., 190.

551. Vera Stravinsky and Robert Craft, *Stravinsky in Pictures and Documents* (London: Hutchinson, 1979), 204.

552. Ralph Vaughan Williams, "A Musical Autobiography," in Hubert Foss, *Ralph Vaughan Williams* (London: Harrap, 1950), 25.

553. "Verdi—A Symposium," *Opera* (London), February 1951, 114–15.

554. Hector Berlioz, *Journal des débats*, 9 February 1860, quoted in Eleanor Perényi, *Liszt* (London: Weidenfeld & Nicolson, 1974), 377.

555. Lillie de Hegermann-Lindencrone, *In the Courts of Memory* (New York,

1911), quoted in *The Book of Musical Anecdotes*, ed. Norman Lebrecht (London: Andre Deutsch, 1985), 107.

556. Emil Naumann, *Italienische Tondichter von Palestrina bis auf die Gegenwart* (Munich, 1876), quoted in *The Book of Musical Anecdotes*, ed. Norman Lebrecht (London: Andre Deutsch, 1985), 107.

557. Herbert Weinstock, *Rossini: A Biography* (London: Oxford University Press, 1968), 284.

558. Ibid., 302.

559. *Robert Schumann: The Man and His Music*, ed. Alan Walker (London: Barrie & Jenkins, 1972), 26.

560. Ibid.

561. Joan Chissell, *Schumann* (London: Dent, 1948), 65.

562. Ibid., 56.

563. Modeste Tchaikovsky, *The Life and Letters of Peter Ilich Tchaikovsky*, ed. and trans. Rosa Newmarch (New York: Vienna House, 1973), vol. 2, 431–32.

564. *Interviews and Encounters with Verdi*, ed. Marcello Conati, trans. Richard Stokes (London: Gollancz, 1984), 328–29.

565. Richard Specht, *Johannes Brahms*, quoted in *The Music Lover's Miscellany*, ed. Eric Blom (London: Gollancz, 1935), 92.

566. J. Lawrence Erb, *Brahms* (London: Dent, 1925), 115.

567. Ibid., 116.

568. Ibid., 116–17.

569. Letter from Cui dated 9 March 1863, quoted in Nicolas Slonimsky, *Lexicon of Musical Invective*, 2d ed. (Seattle: University of Washington Press, 1969), 230–31.

570. Edward Lockspeiser, *Debussy: His Life and Mind* (Cambridge: Cambridge University Press, 1978), 2:68.

571. Ibid.

572. Ernest Newman, *Wagner as Man and Artist* (London: Dent, 1914), 323.

573. M. D. Calvocoressi, *Musicians Gallery* (London: Faber, 1933), 53.

574. Pierre Bernac, *Francis Poulenc: The Man and His Songs* (London: Gollancz, 1977), 34.

575. H. T. Finck, *Massenet and His Operas* (London, 1910), quoted in *The Book of Musical Anecdotes*, ed. Norman Lebrecht (London: Andre Deutsch, 1985), 174.

576. Natalie Bauer-Lechner, *Recollections of Gustav Mahler*, trans. Dika Newlin (London: Faber, 1980), 38.

577. Ibid., 137.

578. Ibid.

579. *A Working Friendship: The Correspondence between Richard Strauss and Hugo von Hofmannsthal*, trans. Hanns Hammelmann and Ewald Moser (New York: Vienna House, 1974), 433.

580. Gerald Abraham, *Rimsky-Korsakov* (London: Duckworth, 1945), 83.

581. Ibid.

582. *Testimony, the Memoirs of Dmitri Shostakovich*, related to and edited by Solomon Volkov (London: Hamish Hamilton, 1979), 157.

583. Erik Tawaststjerna, *Sibelius*, trans. Robert Layton, vol. 1 (London: Faber, 1976), 157; B. Von Törne, *Sibelius: A Close-Up* (London: Faber, 1937).

584. Robert Simpson, *Carl Nielsen, Symphonist* (London: Dent, 1952), 192.

585. Igor Stravinsky, *Igor Stravinsky: An Autobiography* (New York: Norton, 1962), 39.

586. Edward Lockspeiser, *Debussy: His Life and Mind* (Cambridge: Cambridge University Press, 1978), 2:68.

587. Alexander Wheelock Thayer, *Life of Beethoven* (Princeton: Princeton University Press, 1967), 872.

588. Hector Berlioz, *The Memoirs of Hector Berlioz*, trans. David Cairns (London: Panther, 1970), 101–2.

589. John Warrack, *Carl Maria von Weber*, rev. ed. (London: 1976), 280.

590. Edward Lockspeiser, *Debussy: His Life and Mind* (Cambridge: Cambridge University Press, 1978), 2:63.

591. Hector Berlioz, *The Memoirs of Hector Berlioz*, trans. David Cairns (London: Panther, 1970), 123.

592. Robert Simpson, *Carl Nielsen, Symphonist* (London: Dent, 1952), 189.

593. Hélène Jourdan-Morhange, *Ravel et Nous* (Geneva, 1945), 89.

594. Arnold Schoenberg, *Style and Idea,* ed. Leonard Stein, trans. Leo Black (London: Faber, 1984), 483–84.

595. Joan Peyser, *Boulez: Composer, Conductor, Enigma* (London: Cassell, 1977), 50.

596. Ibid., 212.

597. Eric Walter White, *Stravinsky: The Composer and His Works* (London: Faber, 1966), 108.

598. Michael Kennedy, *Britten* (London: Dent, 1981), 121.

599. Louis P. Lochner, *Fritz Kreisler* (New York: Macmillan, 1950), quoted in *The Book of Musical Anecdotes,* ed. Norman Lebrecht (London: Andre Deutsch, 1985), 258.

Index of Composers

Page numbers set in boldface indicate the location of the main entry.

Vaughan Williams, Ralph (1872–
1958): Beethoven, 16, 22; Berlioz,
29; Bizet, 30; Delius, 56; Mahler,
90; Ravel, 118; Verdi, 150
Verdi, Giuseppe (1813–1901), **149–51**;
Beethoven, 21; Bellini, 24; Berlioz,
28; Boito, 32; Gluck, 68; Gounod,
71; Mascagni, 92; Palestrina, 108;
Puccini, 114; Rossini, 121; Wagner,
153–54

Wagner, Richard (1813–1883), **152–57**;
J. S. Bach, 5; Beethoven, 13, 16,
17, 18–19, 20, 21, 22–23, 24; Bellini,
24; Berlioz, 28; Brahms, 36–37;
Bruckner, 41–42; Gluck, 68–69;

Handel, 73–74; Liszt, 86; Mendelssohn, 95; Mozart, 101; Offenbach,
107; Rossini, 121; Verdi, 150
Walton, William (1902–1983): Elgar,
60; Henze, 78
Weber, Carl Maria Von (1786–1826),
158–59; Beethoven, 12–13
Webern, Anton Von (1883–1945),
160–61
Weingartner, Felix (1863–1942): Beethoven, 19
Wellesz, Egon (1885–1974): Schoenberg, 128
Wolf, Hugo (1860–1903), **162**;
Brahms, 37; Bruckner, 42

About the Author

JOHN L. HOLMES is a retired commercial counsellor for the Australian government with a special musicological interest in conductors and their recordings. He has published numerous record reviews and articles on musical subjects, and is the author of *Conductors on Record* (Greenwood Press, 1982) and *Conductors—A Record Collector's Guide* (1988).